JOURNEY TOWARD
WHOLENESS

Justice, Peace and Health
in an Interdependent World

D0109589

JOURNEY TOWARD
WHOLENESS

Justice, Peace and Health in an Interdependent World

Cathie Lyons

Foreword by Dame Nita Barrow

FRIENDSHIP PRESS • NEW YORK

DEDICATION

We are given guides in life: real people who care passionately about the needs of others, who show the way we must go to make love real in a hurting world—people who work tirelessly to make a vision come true. This book is dedicated to the remembrance of one such person:

TISH SOMMERS

co-founder of the Displaced Homemakers Movement
and the Older Women's League

Tish Sommers was a woman with a vision of a just and compassionate society. The way she lived her life made a difference in others' lives—still does and always will.

Library of Congress Cataloging-in-Publication Data

Lyons, Cathie, 1944–
    Journey toward wholeness.

    1. Health—Religious aspects——Christianity. 2. Justice. 3. Love
(Theology) I. Title.
BT732.L96   1987   261.8'321   86-33561
ISBN 0-377-00171-6

Unless otherwise stated, all Bible quotations used in this book are from the
Revised Standard Version, copyright 1946 and 1952 by the Division of Christian Education of the National Council of the Churches of Christ in the
United States of America. Quotations have in certain instances been edited
for inclusive language according to that organization's guidelines.

ISBN 0-377-00171-6

Editorial offices: 475 Riverside Drive, Room 772, New York, NY 10115
Distribution offices: P.O. Box 37844, Cincinnati, OH 45237
Copyright © 1987 by Friendship Press, Inc.
Printed in the United States of America

TABLE OF CONTENTS

FOREWORD ix

INTRODUCTION xi

1. **The Scriptures as the Text of Human Possibility** 1
   To love one another in an interdependent global community . . . 1
   To love one another *by working for justice* in an
   interdependent global community 3
   To love one another by working for justice *and liberation*
   in an interdependent global community 5
   To love one another by working for justice, liberation *and*
   shalom in an interdependent global community 9
   To love one another by working for justice, liberation,
   shalom and reconciliation in an interdepended global
   community 16

2. **Health for All: A Social Goal and a Religious Imperative** . . . 19
   Health for All is a religious imperative grounded in our faith
   in Jesus Christ 19
   Being clear about what Health for All means 22

3. **Health for All Means *Prevention*** 25
   Poor in North America: An older woman's story 25
   How the environments in which we live affect our health 28
   The child-survival revolution: Addressing one of the most
   obvious signs of brokenness in God's created order 35

4. **Health for All Means** *Participation* 49

   Jamkhed, India: A cradle of hope and Health for All 50

   United States women organize to take charge of their health ..59

5. **Health for All Means** *Political Action* 62

   Political action to protect and promote health 62

   Racism, poverty and health status in the U.S. 63

   Urban wealth, rural poverty and international dependency 65

   A worldwide threat to health 68

   Working for the health and wholeness of persons and the
societies in which they live 71

6. **Acquired Immune Deficiency Syndrome (AIDS): A Case-Study for Disease Prevention, Participation and Political Action** 73

   Who is affected by AIDS? 74

   Health education and disease prevention 75

   Community-wide cooperation and participation 76

   The politics of AIDS 77

   The churches and the AIDS crisis 80

7. **The Church as a Healing Community within Nations and the World** 82

   Point of focus: South Africa 83

   The challenge to the church 84

   How shall the churches respond? 88

   Justice: A precondition of health and wholeness for all 89

FOOTNOTES 92

FOREWORD

by Dame Nita Barrow

Health is not simply the absence of disease. Nor is gaining one's health necessarily a matter of medical intervention. Health is no less than a basic human right. That is Cathie Lyons' conviction and it guides every chapter of this important book.

The book is important for several reasons. First, it is based in Christian faith. The author repeatedly shows how health and wholeness are a vital part of the Scriptures. She explains why the Gospel's challenge to liberate the oppressed must be seen to include the liberation of people whose ill health is caused by systemic injustices and poverty.

Lyons has no illusions: She knows that most of the world's medical care is available according to economic and political realities, not human needs. She has seen from nation to nation that health care continues to be centered on cures — often requiring expensive medical technology — rather than on the preventing of disease in the first place. She has seen responsibility for health placed in the hands of specialists, rather than in the hands of people. She knows that even in some developed countries, like the United States, needed health care is reserved for people who can afford it. Lyons says *no* to this. She asks for people's support in changing these unbalanced realities.

This leads to a second reason this book is important. It focuses on people's participation: on their rights and political actions. It focuses on the need for governments to make decisions based on the common good of all persons, so that people can take their destiny into their own hands; can take part in the discussions that affect their health; can shape the quality of their lives and the quality of life in their communities.

A third reason this book is such a valuable resource is that it brings together the perspectives of many different groups in the international health community. Cathie Lyons has long been on the forefront of attempts to express health principles in language people can understand. She has worked to translate the World Health Organization's goal of "Health for All" into terms that speak to people's everyday lives. Her work with the Christian Medical Commission of the World Council of Churches not only reinforced her own thinking but allowed her to interpret with people around the world the need to promote and protect their own health using the best means available to them. Thus the book represents the thinking of concerned working groups around the world. Moreover, it is a very readable synthesis.

Lyons' global emphasis is crucial. In focusing on prevention, participation and political action she uses examples from around the world, from cities in North America to villages in India. Nor is Lyons limited to the conventional scope of what health and wholeness require. The global arms race, the sanctioned oppression of blacks in South Africa and racism everywhere, all are identified as barriers to human wholeness and all require our concerted efforts if real transformation is to come about.

It is evident throughout the pages of this book that the journey toward health and wholeness can accomplish little unless all groups and cultures in every national setting address it together. One part of the world is not "whole", no matter how advanced its health care systems may be, as long as people on another continent or in a neighboring community are ignored in their needless suffering.

Finally, Lyons' book is unique in its emphasis on the strength of the church's role as a healing community. She believes in the tremendously important part Christians can play, not only in ministering to people in need, but in addressing the principalities and powers that keep them in need. She knows that the church is called to a deeper awareness of what it means to be a healing community in order that people who are ill, or who live with handicapping conditions, or who have AIDS, can find the acceptance and sense of worth that they often have been denied in church and society. It is here in the church, too, that people who are disabled or ill are bringing us all to a deeper understanding of what it means to be whole.

Ultimately, *Journey toward Wholeness* is a book about possibility. The possibility that Health for All can be more than a goal, but can be a reality. That people can bring it about. That we can grow in compassion for one another. That we can learn the basic rules of disease prevention for ourselves and our families; can begin to work together to bring about needed changes; can reach a new understanding of what "wholeness" means. It is this wholeness that is God's will for us that Cathie Lyons describes so eloquently in this book.

Dame Nita Barrow is Ambassador and Permanent Representative of Barbados to the United Nations. A professional health educator, Dame Nita was Director of the Christian Medical Commission of the World Council of Churches and is at present one of seven presidents of the WCC. In 1985, Dame Nita was a member of a Commonwealth Eminent Persons Group sent to South Africa to promote dialogue and peaceful change to end apartheid.

INTRODUCTION

The faith-inspired concept of health and wholeness presented in this book does not draw its meaning from the older, still familiar idea of health as the absence of disease or infirmity. Here, the meaning of health and wholeness is intimately related to the process of becoming the persons we are intended to be. In this book, health and wholeness have to do with communal and personal well-being; with persons acting and living in harmony with one another, with God and with all of creation. As such, health and wholeness require the establishment of equitable and just economic, political and social conditions which benefit individuals and the societies in which they live.

The words "health" and "wholeness' have different meanings for different people. Throughout this book they will be shown to be characteristics of persons who live out their faith by creating more just and compassionate societies, who make God's love real in a hurting and broken world.

The first part of the book invites readers to use the scriptures as the text of human possibility. The gospels reveal the inseparability of love for God and love for one's neighbor. In fact, the great commission Jesus gave his followers was that they love God with all their heart, mind and soul—and their neighbor as themselves. These chapters show how love for God is lived out in concrete human encounters, in taking on personal and social responsibilities, in working to bring about health and wholeness through justice, liberation, *shalom* and reconciliation.

This book will also introduce a concept that must be central to any just and compassionate society: the goal of Health for All. Through the framework of this goal we will see the situations of need that affect so many of the world's people, including significant numbers of persons in the United States and Canada. The goal of Health for All also provides the opportunities for actions which promote health, prevent disease and lead to community-wide participation and political action.

The goal of Health for All was articulated worldwide in 1977 by the World Health Organization, an intergovernmental body of the United Nations. Much of its inspiration, however, came from the churches. The Christian Medical Commission of the Geneva-based World Council of Churches, at that time under the leadership of Dame Nita Barrow, spoke a clear word of conscience about the suffering of millions of people—needless suffering born of poverty, injustice, social and political neglect. Suffering that the churches—and the conscience of the world—could tolerate no longer.

Today, the goal of Health for All represents one of the most important social challenges of the twentieth century and of the centuries to come.

For the churches, the question is not: Can the goal be accomplished? but rather: Are churches doing all they can to make the goal a reality? The goal offers untold opportunities for churches to speak a prophetic word in the world, to work cooperatively with other churches and faiths, and, with governmental and non-governmental organizations, to respond to both human suffering and human hope.

The second part of this book highlights ways in which political, social and economic factors dramatically affect the well-being of individuals and the communities in which they live. It shows why churches and persons of faith must address not only what individuals need and can do to protect and promote their own health, but how churches must also address vast collective realities: the wars, racism, poverty, oppression and exploitation which perpetuate needless suffering and death on a massive scale.

Health and wholeness mean being engaged with people, building communities of conscience, reaching beyond one's self for the good of others, creating more just and compassionate societies.

This book is one step in the search, one voice of concern and protest about the needless and unjust suffering of so many—suffering with which we are all in complicity, whether as part of its root cause or as silent, unmoved onlookers. This writing is intended to stand alongside the voices of others: of women and men who cry out for a better life for their children; of theologians and laypeople who work for the liberation of their lands from all forms of oppression; of persons who are in prison or who have been martyred because they stood against injustice; of adults, children and youth everywhere who care that the lives of individuals, families, communities and entire regions are being torn apart by violence, greed, poverty, racism and homelessness. All these voices reflect people's intense yearnings for health and wholeness, and the commitment of so many to work against great odds to make these yearnings come true.

The journey toward health and wholeness is a journey of involvement, of contact, seeing, hearing, touching, being willing to suffer with and for others. It requires taking sides with the God who takes sides against the causes of alienation, injustice and war. Ultimately, the experience of health and wholeness comes as a part of the journey itself. It is a part of living the life Jesus has shown us how to live.

This book is an invitation to take up the journey, to engage in dialogue, to rethink old answers, to join together in faith and action and in so doing, to begin to experience the health and wholeness which God intends for our lives and for all persons.

—CATHIE LYONS
New York City
July 1986

1. THE SCRIPTURES AS THE TEXT OF HUMAN POSSIBILITY

The scriptures are ancient yet their importance is timeless for they serve as a guidebook about the ways of the God who is constantly present in the human journey, instilling every moment with hope and meaning, with opportunities for growth, liberation and newness of life.

The scriptures are also a sourcebook of stories about people's errant ways: about the oppression of some by others; about being lost in the love of riches and power; about faithlessness and the worship of false gods; about the need to be set free from captivity.

The scriptures give shape to the different ways men and women are invited to live as followers of Jesus Christ, a man whose life exemplified faithfulness, servanthood and selfless love, whose example gives new proportion to our lives. The new life to which we are called is filled with religious and social significance. It is a life of prayer, action and engagement with others to establish just and loving communities in which God's intentions for the world can be realized.

Using the scriptures as the text of human possibility, we are able to gain a vision of what we are to do in these disturbing times to make health and wholeness a reality.

To love one another in an interdependent global community

> *An old rabbi once asked his students how one could recognize when night ends and day begins. "Is it when, from a great distance, you can tell a dog from a sheep?" one student asked. "No," said the rabbi. "Is it when, from a great distance, you can tell a date palm from a fig tree?" another student asked. "No," said the rabbi. "Then when is it?" the students asked. "It is when you look into the face of any human creature and see your brother or your sister there. Until then, night is still with us."*
>
> The Strength of the Weak, *by Dorothee Soelle*

Is night still with us? Or is this the dawning of a new day in which we respond to the human community as one family of God?

We are all created in the image of God. We are all children of one Creator. We are brothers and sisters and neighbors of one another. Love for the neighbor who lives in Salina, Kansas or in Delhi, India or in the Luboa bantustan in South Africa's northern Transvaal, whom we may or may not ever meet—this love is central to our biblical heritage and to the health and wholeness which is God's will for us.

For Jesus Christ, health and wholeness was a way of life lived loving others the way God loved him. Learning to love the way Jesus has shown us how is essential to our realization of what health and wholeness are, and to our making this love our way of life. "God's way of wholeness for the individual, through Jesus, is love. Loving our enemies, doing good to those who persecute us, turning the other cheek, walking the second mile—these are not legal obligations. They are powerful truths that transform the evil and destructiveness that would destroy us.''[1]

The scriptures speak also of the love people who say they love God are to have for one another. The first commission given to Jesus' followers was that they love God with heart, soul and mind—and their neighbor as themselves. The love which we are to have for one another is to take very concrete form, as seen in the Gospel according to Matthew (25:30–46), where the hungry are given food to eat, drink is provided to the person who is thirsty, those who are sick or in prison are visited, the stranger is invited in, and the one who is naked is clothed.

An upcoming chapter describes the situation of a woman named Sheila Bond. Through her story it becomes clear that the phrase "Health for All" is not merely an international health organization's slogan about the needs of faceless masses of people. These words voice a concern about real people—people whose personal, social and economic needs directly affect their health and wholeness. Mrs. Bond lives in every community in every country on earth. She is the neighbor who is in need. She is the human creature walking the road, in the rabbi's story, in whose face people of faith are challenged to see the sister, the brother. To love one another the way the gospels call us to love we must address Mrs. Bond's very complex needs within the context of her very concrete situation.

What is the opposite of loving one another? The answer might be: "hating one another". But the other side of love is much more pervasive than hatred. It is indifference. Being unaffected by what is going on around us. It is the absence of any feeling of oneness with those who move around us. It means not exposing ourselves to the situation of the other person. It is self-imposed, selective alienation, separation. It is indifference to injustice except as injustice affects our own lives.

The opposite of love is lack of concern about those without jobs as long as one can hold on to one's own job. It is not caring that persons who are poor cannot receive the services they need as long as one can get care for one's own sick child. It is the indifference that comes when one loses sight of the inherent worth of every person.

The opposite of love for one another is a situation in which religion does not exist. "Religion interprets rather than just observes. Religion does not confirm that there are hungry people in the world; it interprets the hungry to be our brethren whom we allow to starve."[2] The opposite of loving one another is denying God in our lives. " 'God' is the name we give to that voice in us which summons us to go beyond ourselves."[3]

2

The German theologian Dorothee Soelle has written that love for one another is central to our faith and our lives. "The essence of the Gospel is contained in the idea that we should love each other, contained in this amazingly simple and banal principle."[4]

When we look at this principle in the context of the world in which we live, we find a troubling reality: Across the world, many people are starving. Many more are persistently hungry. Hundreds of thousands are uprooted, fleeing war and civil strife or driven out by rural poverty. Others are left homeless on the streets of the wealthiest nations of the world and some who need care are turned away at hospital doors because they cannot pay to get in. Whole regions thirst for clean water. Mothers watch naked children die from want of simple, basic things. Young people, brothers and sisters, mothers and fathers fighting for justice in different regions of the world are detained, locked in prisons and tortured for their just and loving beliefs.

These realities, which circumscribe millions of lives, are as much the concern of the gospel today as they were in the time of Jesus. How, then, are we to love one another in this interdependent global community? How do we relate this essence of the gospel—the need to love one another—to all of society's structures? How are we to shape our personal lives in accordance with this central message? How can we develop this message? Teach it to our children? Live it out in the tasks that face our generation?[5]

Part of the answer lies in doing the work of justice. For just as we show our love for God by loving our neighbor, we love our neighbor by working for justice. Too often, when we read in Matthew about providing clothing, shelter, food and water, we think of personal acts of love, not acts of justice.

To love one another *by working for justice* in an interdependent global community

"God has told you what is good . . . and what does the Sovereign One require of you but to do justice, to love kindness and to walk humbly with your God?" (Micah 6:7–8)

Professor Soelle writes that "Biblical texts are best read with a pair of glasses made out of today's newspaper."[6] The text she is concerned with is Isaiah 58:6–12:

Is not this the fast that I choose:
   to loose the bonds of wickedness,
   to undo the thongs of the yoke,
to let the oppressed go free,
   and to break every yoke?
Is it not to share your bread with the hungry,
   and bring the homeless poor into your house;

when you see the naked, to provide cover
and not to hide yourself from your own flesh?
Then shall your light break forth like the dawn.
and your healing shall spring up speedily;
your righteousness shall go before you,
the glory of God shall be your rear guard.
Then you shall call, and God will answer;
you shall cry, and God will say, Here I am.
If you take away from the midst of you the yoke,
the pointing of the finger, and speaking wickedness,
if you pour yourself out for the hungry
and satisfy the desire of the afflicted,
then shall your light rise in the darkness
and your gloom be as the noonday.
And God will guide you continually,
and satisfy your desire with good things,
and make your bones strong;
And you shall be like a watered garden,
like a spring of water,
whose waters fail not.
And your ancient ruins shall be rebuilt;
you shall raise up the foundations of many generations;
you shall be called the repairer of the breach,
the restorer of streets to dwell in.

Soelle states it well: "Isaiah sees what is happening among his people and in his society. He sees people unjustly imprisoned; he sees people abused and oppressed, sees them suffer from violence."[7] The text is not only about the injustices being committed, but about what will happen to those who seek to put an end to the wrongdoing, who loose the bonds of wickedness, who let the oppressed go free. In the lyrical style of the prophets, Isaiah reminds the reader that one who does these just things will reap great goodness in return. The doer of righteousness will become rich—but not, as Soelle points out, in material things. "The text speaks to the richness of life. Do not be sparing of yourself, it says. The more of yourself you expend, the richer you become." The riches here are "the riches of being human, not the riches of owning things." This text from Isaiah "suggests to us the possibility of living a different life."

To love one another by working for justice is to live a different kind of life: a life of total engagement with and for others. Sometimes it means sharing the bread we have with those who are hungry. But it also means working to change that which makes some people poor while others have wealth, that which keeps some people afflicted while others are untouched by illness or by need.

In Chapter Four of this book the story is told of Jamkhed, India,

4

which is a cradle of hope, wholeness and justice because of the innovative health care system begun by mission doctors Raj and Mabelle Arole. The Aroles knew from the outset that if they treated people's illnesses without working with them to change the conditions which made and kept them ill, they would not be acting justly. The suffering of some would be relieved for a while, but the time would come when the same people would return. All they would have done would have been to foster dependency, to keep the yoke of illness around people's necks.

However, the Aroles provide a poignant example of what it means to love one another by working for justice. Raj Arole's words about the village people with whom he works makes this clear: "The Lord chose simple people to be his disciples. He demonstrated that God loves and respects every person we move with. God has endowed every human being with potential. We are challenged to help persons achieve this potential for the health and development of themselves and the communities where they live." In working for justice with the village people, the Aroles saw them become freed from the burdens of poverty, ignorance and illness; they saw them begin to realize lives of God-given possibility.

Another example of loving one another by working for justice is described in the story Sithembiso Nyoni tells about the people she works with in Zimbabwe. Ms. Nyoni is working to bring about fundamental changes in the lives of those who live in poverty. The foci of her attention are the forces that create and perpetuate rural poverty locally, regionally, nationally and internationally.

Think about the growing number of hungry and homeless people in the United States and Canada. Who are they in your community? What systemic factors make their situation what it is? What caused it? What keeps it going? How is the cycle of poverty, hunger, homelessness to be broken? How are the fetters to be loosened?

To love one another in an interdependent global community means that we in the world faith community must translate the words of Micah: to do justice, to love kindness, to walk humbly with God—within the context of the world in which we live. The words of the prophets remind us that when one's religion is lived out for and with one's neighbor, the religious response becomes one of protest. Protest against all that keeps people in desperate need, struggling to survive and to stay well. When we do what Micah tells us God asks us to do, "love for the neighbor" is translated into religious, political and social action.

To love one another by working for justice *and liberation* in an interdependent global community

The Spirit of God is upon me,
Because God annointed me to preach
the Gospel to the poor.

5

God has sent me to proclaim release
  to the captives,
And recovery of sight to the blind,
To set free those who are downtrodden.
                              Luke 4:18

"God, through his prophet Jesus, acts in history by preaching good news to the poor, the liberation of the captives, the setting at liberty of those who are oppressed. In so doing Jesus also reveals God's central judgement against the rich and the powerful, the religious and the social elites. The liberation of the poor becomes the central locus of God's action in history. God opts for the poor in order to right the wrongs in history."[8]

The liberation theologies being written today are fired in the crucible of the human struggle against evil and oppression. These theologies are true to the message of the Christ whom we confess as our Sovereign and Savior: who came to set the captives free, to release us from bondage to sin—and true to Christ crucified, who was hung on a cross among thieves whom he invited to enter the kingdom of heaven; whom we confess as a person of peace.

In the words of Rosemary Ruether, "liberation theology wishes to reintegrate spirituality and material life. It seeks to overcome dualisms which have been traditional in Christian thought, but which are, in fact, foreign to biblical spirituality: the dualisms between faith and life, prayer and action and daily work, contemplation and struggle, creation and salvation. For liberation theologians sin means not only alienation from God and personal brokenness of life, but also the structural evils of war, racism, sexism, and economic exploitation which allow some people to dehumanize others. Likewise, salvation means not only reconciliation with God and personal amendment of life, but a commitment to a struggle for a transformed social order where all these evils will be overcome."[9]

In both the Old and New Testaments God is revealed as a liberator, intervening in human political and social history. In the story of the Exodus, God hears the lamentations and cries of a people; God cares that people suffer from oppression. God spoke to Moses, telling him to take to the Israelites the word that God would set them free from bondage. In the Exodus, God is revealed as one who takes sides, bringing deliverance to the oppressed. (Exodus 6:2–9).

Archbishop Desmond Tutu has written about the "concreteness of the Exodus liberation. It was a thoroughly political act by which God was first made known to the Israelites. Nothing could be more political than helping a group of slaves to escape from their bondage. For the Israelites, therefore, the liberation of the Exodus was not just a spiritual or mystical experience. It was highly materialistic and had to do with

6

being protected from an enemy in pursuit, being fed when hungry, being provided with water to quench their thirst. But it also had to do with the religious and spiritual dimension of forging relationships with God. They owed their very being to God and were bound in a covenant relationship . . . that excluded worship of other deities."[10]

Archbishop Tutu reminds the readers of his book *Hope and Suffering* that the theme of liberation and deliverance is as characteristic of the New Testament as it is of the Old. In the New Testament, "it refers to the forgiveness of sins, to recovery of health, to the feeding of the hungry. People are set free from bondage to the world, the Devil and sin, in order to be free for God."[11] In the New Testament we are set free to live by the example of Jesus Christ; set free from all that would make us less than God intends us to be; set free to measure our lives by nothing less than the life of Jesus, "a compassionate, a caring person, concerned more for others than for himself, ready to demonstrate his love . . . by laying down his life."[12] In the New Testament, liberation is total. "It includes being set free from political, social and economic structures that are oppressive and unjust since these would enslave us, and make us less than God intends us to be."[13]

What, then, is asked of persons of faith in the words that begin this section: "To love one another by working for justice *and liberation* in an interdependent global community"? On this critical matter, Archbishop Tutu is specific: "In setting us free to be God's children, God wants to enlist us . . . as co-workers in the business of the Kingdom (1 Corinthians 3:9); we are to labor with God to humanize the universe."[14]

The work of establishing God's kingdom on earth here and now means that "There is nowhere that the writ of God does not run, for everything belongs to God (Psalm 24:1). Caesar must be accorded what is appropriate for him, and God must have all—including Caesar's domain; otherwise there would be a part of the universe, of life, which did not fall under God's control."[15]

Third world liberation theologians are very specific about the meaning of liberation and the work of further establishing God's kingdom in current situations in which so many are oppressed by the wealth and power of so few. Think for a moment about the following facts and statements drawn from chapters in this book:

• Forty thousand children die needlessly each day from preventable diseases and illnesses in the countries of the third world.
• Last year alone, the fifteen million young children who died in the third world is the equivalent of the entire under-five population of the United States. On a European scale, it is as if the combined under-five populations of Britain, France, Italy, Spain and the Federal Republic of Germany were wiped out in one year.

- In Pakistan, maternal deaths in one month are equal to the maternal deaths in one year in North America, Europe, Australia and Japan combined.
- Every day, decision-makers make policy in favor of the urban centers and large health institutions where only a few can be attended to. They choose to invest in arms instead of agricultural implements to produce more food. They choose to sell land to multinational corporations to produce cotton, coffee, tobacco, maize, or flowers for export before distributing land to the rural poor who need to grow food to feed their families and to sell for cash.
- For America's poor, the infant mortality rate is up. And the infant mortality rate gap between the rural poor and the rest of the nation grew an alarming thirty-nine percent between 1981 and 1983.
- In the United States, the gap between upper-income and low-income families was wider in 1984 than at any time since Census began collecting these data in 1947.
- In 1985, of all young black children in the United States, over fifty percent lived in poverty—the highest poverty rate every recorded in that rich nation.
- Persistent and troubling interrelationships continue to exist between racism, poverty, health care and health status in the United States.
- The world's annual military spending is eight hundred billion dollars. That's two billion each day, $100 million each hour, one and one-half million dollars each minute, $25,000 every second. The cost of a half-day's world armaments spending could pay for the full immunization of all the children in the world against the common infectious diseases.
- Consider the situation in South Africa: "On the one hand are those who benefit from the status quo, who are determined to maintain it at any cost. On the other hand are those who do not benefit in any way from the situation as it is now, who are treated as mere labor units, moved about like cattle and dumped in 'homelands' to starve—all for the benefit of the privileged minority." (From the Kairos Document; see page 85.)
- The causes of ill health—and the things that block the road to good health—are rooted in every part of society and ultimately, in politics. The political and economic changes needed to bring health to all cannot easily be sidestepped.

As individuals and faith communities seek to end their complicity with oppression, and work with those who are oppressed to remove the injustices that cause so many to suffer, the kingdom of God breaks in. Rosemary Ruether states it eloquently: "Closeness to the kingdom is a matter of concrete reality. . . of discerning the realities of bondage and the realities of liberation that are actually taking place."[16] She uses an example from Latin America, where the chronic poor health of rural families is often directly related to their landlessness: "In our present world, when we see a society where a few rich families own almost all the land, where they suppress all protest with guns and tanks, where they manipulate religion and education to justify this exploitation, there we are far from the kingdom. But when we see the vast majority rising up against these evils, overthrowing the police state, beginning to create a new society where the hngry are fed, and the poor are able to participate in the decisions that govern their lives, there the kingdom has come close."

Ruether, like all those who work for liberation—whether in Latin America, Zimbabwe, South Africa, India, the Philippines or in the United States and Canada—stresses without reservation that "it is possible to make societies which are more liberating and less oppressive. To deny this is to deny all efficacy to God in history, to make the world solely the kingdom of Satan."

The liberation for which the followers of Christ are called to work in our interdependent global community is none other than that of moving "human society a little farther from the kingdom of Satan, the kingdom of alienation and oppression, and closer to God's kingdom, a society of peace, justice and mutuality." A similar interpretation can be drawn from Dorothea Soelle's writings, in which working for liberation expresses "our hunger for justice and for participation in the kingdom of God."[17] "The Christian answer to the question of meaning is that 'God is love', and this general statement finds concrete expression in...experiences of liberation."[18]

To love one another by working for justice, liberation *and shalom* in an interdependent global community

At the very heart of the Old Testament is the testimony to shalom, *that marvelous Hebrew word which means peace. But the peace which is* shalom *is not negative or one-dimensional. It is much more than the absence of war. It is positive peace: harmony, wholeness, health, and well-being in all human relationships. It is the natural state of humanity as birthed by God. It is harmony between humanity and all of God's good creation. All of creation is interrelated. Every creature, every element, every force of nature participates in the whole of Creation. If any person is denied* shalom, *all are thereby diminished.*

Shalom, then, is the sum total of moral and spiritual qualities in a community whose life is in harmony with God's good creation. It indicates an alternative community: an alternative to the idolatries, oppression and violence which mark the ways of many nations.

Swords into plowshares, arms converted into food and death to life, no more wars or training for wars, peaceable kingdoms, joy and peace such that the trees clap their hands, new covenants written on the heart: these are the radiant images of shalom *at the visionary heights of Old Testament prophecy. With them we know that the Bible is really one Book: they forecast the coming of the One who will be the Prince of Peace.*

And so He comes. He comes heralded by angels who sing: "Glory to God and peace on Earth!" He invokes the most special blessings upon peacemakers. He exalts the humanity of aliens. He commands us to love our enemies, for He knows, even if we do not, that if we hate our enemies we blind and destroy ourselves. Shalom, after all, is the heart of God and the law of Creation. It cannot be broken with impunity.[19]

In the journey toward wholeness we are called to take responsibility for the way we live. "Our health, our wholeness is partly a function of our willingness to be responsible for the *way* we live as the children of God."[20] We live in an interdependent global community where our actions can affect the enhancement or the total destruction of all creation.

It is painful to change, and it involves taking risks—daring to risk danger as we are called to conversion and wholeness. Conversion means letting God touch every part of us. The call is to allow God to lovingly redeem and liberate us from our worst deeply-ingrained habit patterns.[21]

War and preparations for war, squandering money to build and perfect weapons systems, basic training in how to kill—all these have become deeply-ingrained habit patterns of peoples and nations across the world. Security through the stockpiling of nuclear arms has become the contemporary false idol of our nations. But nuclear weapons cannot secure security. They cannot create lasting peace in the world. Never could. Never will.

Out of grave concern over the nuclear arms race, the Council of Bishops of the (U.S.) United Methodist Church, in 1985, prepared a pastoral letter and a Foundation Document, "In Defense of Creation: The Nuclear Arms Crisis and a Just Peace". They did this as a prophetic response to the Word of God and to their understanding of that Word at this moment in history.

Holding firm to the conviction that "there is no just cause which can warrant the waging of nuclear war or any use of nuclear weapons" and that "deterrence must no longer receive the churches' blessing, even as a temporary warrant for the maintenance of nuclear weapons", "In Defense of Creation" catalogues how deeply the arms race tears at the nature and fabric of all human relationships—political, economic or social—on planet Earth. Its inescapable theme is the preciousness of human life and the ways in which life in the United States' inner cities and across the world is being sacrificed while nuclear technology and nuclear animosities are nurtured. The document begins and ends with an affirmation of reverence for life: "In the *shalom* of God's good creation, every person of every race in every nation is a sacred being, made in God's image, and entitled to life and peace, health and freedom."

Within the world today the governments of two superpowers—the United States and the Soviet Union—place their trust for national security in nuclear deterrence. But what makes for real security? The struggle for arms parity between two nations? Or the guarantee of things more basic and fundamental to human growth and development? Consider the image of Jesus weeping before the Jerusalem, the Holy City:

> *There is a stark and sorrowful moment when Jesus, approaching Jerusalem from the neighboring heights, pauses to weep. And why does he weep? He foresees a terrible day of judgment when the Holy City itself will be totally leveled to rubble and dust without "one stone upon another". Why? Because the people there, even the most religious people in that supposedly sacred city, did not really know "the things that make for peace" (Luke 19:41–44). The moment is a powerful intimation of what false security policies based upon weapons of mass destruction can lead to.*
>
> —*"In Defense of Creation"*

The requirements of genuine security are many. Among other things, "security requires economic strength and stability, environmental and public health, educational quality, public confidence, global cooperation." And yet, are not these basic requirements precisely what are most jeopardized through nuclear deterrence ideology and military spending?

The nuclear arms race is a fundamental social justice issue. It has profound domestic and international implications. "In Defense of Creation" states that "The U.S. military buildup between 1980 and 1985 has cost $1.2 trillion. . . . U.S. arms are now being purchased with food stamps, welfare checks, rent subsidies, Medicaid payments, school lunches, and nutrition supplements for poor mothers and their children. Half of the nation's black children and two-fifths of all Hispanic children now live in poverty."

The nuclear arms race between the United States and the Soviet Union touches every continent and every struggle of people in developing countries. The arms race turns "every North-South issue of economic and social justice into an East-West issue of confrontation. It is a major source of injustice to the world's poorest people, whether through squandering of resources, neglect, repression, exploitation, proxy wars, nuclear arrogance, or failure to construct the institutions of multilateral cooperation required for development."

Jesus wept over the Holy City knowing that the people did not know the things that make for peace. Justice is one of the things that makes for peace, and the *shalom* of God is denied each time justice is withheld. "In *shalom* there is no contradiction between justice and peace, or between peace and security, or between love and justice." (Isaiah 32:16, Jeremiah 29:7)

The *shalom* of God "discloses an alternative community to the idolatries, oppressions, and violence which mark the ways of many nations. The nuclear crisis is not primarily a matter of missiles: it is a crisis of human community." Peacemaking is a sacred call. "The Church of Jesus Christ, in the power and unity of the Holy Spirit, is called to serve as an alternative community to an alienated and fractured world: a loving and peaceable international company of disciples transcending all governments, races, and ideologies, reaching out to all 'enemies', ministering to all the victims of poverty and oppression."

Called, then, to love one another by working for *shalom,* what can persons of faith do to show the moral and spiritual qualities which exist when life is lived in harmony with God? How can we take responsibility for the way we live in an interdependent global community? How can we work for the justice which is a requisite for peace among nations?

One thing the ecumenical faith community can do is be united in prayer and action: to become a penitential church of all believers, ministering in the midst of conflict on the side of the poor and the oppressed.

In James 4:1 the question is asked as to the source of quarrels between people. "There follows a catalogue of human sins: excess passion, covetousness, pride, arrogance, evil judgments against brother and neighbor." Ephesians 2:14–19 states that Christ has ordained a ministry of reconciliation and has taught that repentance prepares the way for reconciliation. Repentence, then, must be a task of the church—a prerequisite of reconciliation whether for individuals, groups, nations or churches. The churches' own implication in militarism, racism, sexism and materialism requires a deeply penitent approach to peacemaking."

Another task of the church is to grow in deeper understanding of Jesus as the Prince of Peace who sided with the poor. The world church of people called to be peacemakers can thus "share a strong moral presumption against violence, killing and warfare, seeking every possible means of peaceful conflict resolution." The world church can also address governments, registering concern that "every policy of government must be an act of justice and must be measured by its impact on the poor, the weak, and the oppressed."

Throughout both Testaments, there is a dual attitude toward political authority. The powers of government are legitimate expressions of the Creation's natural order of political community among God's children, as well as constraints upon human sinfulness. Their authority is thus from God—at least provisionally. Rulers are ordinarily to be obeyed. Taxes are ordinarily to be paid. But the moral law implanted in Creation transcends the laws of any state or empire. When governors themselves become oppressive and lawless, when they presume to usurp the sovereignty which belongs to God alone, they are rightfully subject to criticism, correction, and ultimately, resistance.

Loyalty to one's own government is always subject to the transcendent loyalty which belongs to the Sovereign God alone. Such loyalty may be politically expressed either in support of or opposition to current government policies.

—"In Defense of Creation"

Dr. Mamphela Ramphele of South Africa has written that in her country a generation of children is growing up for whom death has lost its sting. It is these children grown tired of oppression and racism, who have taken to the streets armed with nothing more than bricks and angry words of protest. During the imposed states of emergency in 1985 and 1986 the black children of South Africa met resistance in the form of tanks, troop carriers, armed soldiers and teargas-spewing vehicles. Tanks against children. Not to keep the peace, but to defend and protect the policies of a tyrannical government. The black children of South Africa share their violence-ridden childhood with millions of children and youth in the Middle East, Northern Ireland, parts of East Asia and Central America who have never known peace.

Conventional and nuclear weapons proliferate like opulent foliage in the landscape of regional and international hostilities. Against this landscape, hundreds of thousands of people seek refuge from war-torn lives. It is a world of families who live with empty larders, inadequate housing, unsafe water supplies, no sanitary facilities, flies swarming everywhere, ravaged by malnourishment and easily-preventable diseases.

Shalom means the absence of war and civil conflict, of course; it means the end of preparations for war. But *shalom* encompasses much more. *Shalom* is positive peace—peace wherein justice exists. *Shalom* means enough food for all. It means land equitably distributed for the use and benefit of the world's people. It means education. It means that families have enough income. It means freedom from the burdens of preventable illness. It means the establishment of communities, regions, nations and a world in which peace—with justice—is unmolested by oppressors. It means governments committed to protecting the common good.

Shalom means harmony between people and the land, the forest, the sky and the seas. Living *shalom* means valuing oneself, one another and all of God's creation—a creation instilled with goodness that is not to be violated or used for selfish purposes. *Shalom* means that all people take responsibility for the way they live in human community as the people of God. *Shalom* is found in the wholeness of God's creation. Denied to some, it exists for no one.

None of the stories or facts presented in this book are unaffected by

Shalom means positive peace, the absence of war and civil strife, and much much more: food to meet the needs of all, land equitably distributed, education, sufficient family incomes, clean water, participation in all decisions which affect one's life, protection of the common good of all....

WHO – J. Littlewood

WHO – P. Almasy

United Methodist Board of Global Ministries

United Methodist Board of Global Ministries

United Nations: John Isaac

United Methodist Board of Global Ministries

the costs of the arms race. As Victor Sidel says to people concerned about world health and the arms race: "Set a metronome at a rate of one beat per second. Listen to it, remembering that with each beat (each second) the world spends $25,000 in military arms, and that tiny fractions of that spending—over a few hours, one half day, one day, three days—could produce remarkable changes in health and living conditions, especially among the world's poor." Study the words of Rosemary Ruether: "In our present world . . . we see a society where a few rich families own almost all the land, where they suppress all protest with guns and tanks, where they manipulate religion and education to justify this exploitation."

When will we decide for peace with justice—for the *shalom* of God's good creation? When will we be reconciled with God, reconciled as peoples and nations?

To love one another by working for justice, liberation, *shalom and reconciliation* in an interdependent global community

> *We cannot be transformed unless we surrender ourselves to God in every sphere of our existence: the physical, the psychological and spiritual as well as the social, economic and political. We can then experience a change in all our relationships as we turn away from our contemporary idols.*
>
> *—"The Call to Wholeness"*

Why are we more concerned about what will happen to property values if persons who are homeless or mentally-retarded are provided housing in our neighborhood than we are about the fact that our communities shut these people out, discriminate against them, keep them in need and on the fringes of society?

Why is it not possible to secure the funds that are required to carry out the child-survival revolution—so that at least half of the forty thousand child lives now lost each day could be saved? What set of values do we follow when we sign defense contracts guaranteeing payment for years to come for the construction of strategic weapons when we are not sure from one year to the next whether adequate cost-of-living increases will be afforded the elderly?

The World Health Organization estimates that little more than two hundred drugs are "essential"—meaning basic, indispensable and necessary—to any nation's health needs. It states that many of these drugs could be produced locally, stimulating the indigenous economy and marketed at a price everyone in the country could afford. For what purpose, then, and for whose benefit are more than fifteen thousand drug products on the market in many developing nations—at great expense to those countries' national health budgets?

Dorothee Soelle does not answer these questions, but writes pointedly about how such concerns relate to our faith:

> *"We must change direction and return. In order to learn we must first unlearn . . . In order to find meaning we must change our mind. Turn about! Choose a different road! Challenge the goals that have become so accepted that they are never questioned any more. Life is a returning, is conversion. Living means turning about . . . The scale of values in our society is based on the model of continuous progress."*

But how must we really progress? In order to progress, *"we must change direction and return.*

> *"Christianity proclaims not progress but a returning. The most direct route does not continue in the familiar direction, but calls for turning-about-on-your-heel.*
>
> *"Without a change in the direction of our lives, everything will continue as before. We shall continue to pursue the aims to which we have become accustomed, we shall cling to what we have, we shall run in the same direction blind to everything that is happening about us and deaf to the voices of those whose life we destroy. I mean the poor, as threatened by starvation as ever."* [22]
>
> *"Turn about! Break up your fallow ground! From what must we convert, and to what? I think that can be said in simple words: the system under which we live is based on money and power."* [23]

The central work of Jesus was to bring about reconciliation between God and humanity, between us and all others (2 Corinthians 5:19). The direction of reconciliation is return. Return to the will of God and to doing the work of God. And the task of returning continues. So that what is broken can be restored. What is intended can be realized.

Jesus' entire life was a model of what needs to be done for created life to be reconciled with the Creator and with all of creation. In this regard, the way he lived his life is inseparable from his vision of the kingdom of God. As Rosemary Ruether writes: "The kingdom of God is a holistic vision of this world, the created world as it is supposed to be when, as Jesus said, 'God's will is done on earth'. It means both reconciliation with God, when people obey God from the heart, *and* justice on earth and harmony between humanity and nature. These are not two different things, but, in fact, two sides of the same thing. There is no possibility of divorcing the two sides from each other. Reconciliation with God means the revolutionizing of human, social, political relations, overthrowing unjust, oppressive relationships. The socio-political is never lost in Hebrew messianism, but always remains the central expression of what it means to obey God." [24]

To return. To unlearn. To change direction. To let go of contemporary gods. To choose a different road. To obey God from the heart. To do justice. To live a life of engagement with others and for others. To renounce all things that take precedence over love for one another. To live lives of God-given possibility. To do nothing that denies such fulfillment to others. To be *shalom* people. To recognize sin not simply as personal, but as social, collective and institutional.

At every moment, God addresses us as social beings embedded in socio-political and economic systems. God calls us to band together, to seek a transformed society capable of promoting and sustaining peace with justice, health and wholeness for all. God calls us to work against historical human evil. God calls us to experience reconciliation in this time and place by working to establish "the proper conditions of life with God and one another here on earth within the limits of mortal existence."[25]

Every experience in life offers us opportunity for reconciliation. Every movement toward health and wholeness expands our vision of human need and human possibility. Everything in this book speaks about human need—the needs of individuals, communities and societies, of a world in which so many are so poor, living under the heavy mantle of injustice and oppression. For ours is a world in which all persons know loss of faith, suffering and despair of one sort or another.

The scriptures invite us to be healed, to be made whole through living as Jesus has shown us how to live. It is through God's love for us and through Jesus' example of how we are to love one another that health and wholeness are to be found.

The meaning of health which is inspired by faith cannot be defined simply as the absence of disease or illness any more than wholeness means the absence of a handicapping condition. For Jesus Christ, health and wholeness was *a way of life loving others* the way God loved him. Jesus' life is the definition of health and wholeness for those who believe in and follow him.

2. HEALTH FOR ALL: A SOCIAL GOAL AND A RELIGIOUS IMPERATIVE

The theologian Krister Stendahl has said that God's agenda includes the mending of creation. Not only does God invite us to be co-workers in the mending of creation; God enables us, through our life in Christ, to discover those places where brokenness exists and shows us, through Christ's example, the way to make things whole.

Some of the most obvious signs of brokenness are revealed through global health statistics. As the end of the twentieth century nears, hundreds of millions of people endure totally unacceptable states of health. It is because of this tragic reality that the goal of Health for All is so important.

In 1977, the nations of the world affirmed Health for All as the most important social goal to work for by the end of the century. For persons of faith, the goal has an even deeper significance, for in a theological sense, Health for All describes God's hope for the world. And all are invited to take part, to be of a new mind and spirit about what health requires.

Health for All is a religious imperative grounded in our faith in Jesus Christ

The seeds of hope which can make Health for All a reality are found in our faith. For this goal is a covenant in which secular and religious concerns intersect. It is a protest against everything that stands in the way of the fullness of life Jesus proclaimed. It is an affirmation that God's will will be accomplished.

Health for All is about the kingdom of God. "The kingdom, for whose coming Jesus taught us to pray, is defined quite simply as 'God's will done on earth'. God's will done on earth means the fulfillment of people's basic human physical and social needs. . . . The kingdom means conquest of human historical evil; the setting up of proper conditions of human life with God and one another here on earth within the limits of mortal existence."[26]

For the churches, the goal of Health for All points to Jesus' love. This love, which opens persons to respond fully to the needs of others, is the motivating factor for health ministries and social outreach. By his life and example, Jesus taught that the purest expression of God's love is solidarity with all who suffer and are in need. Guided by this faith, the goal of Health for All interprets any person who is hungry or ill to be one's neighbor. Thus the root causes of the neighbor's suffering become critical concerns of churches throughout the world.

The goal also offers a "vision of a this-worldly era of peace and justice"[27] in which religious and secular institutions recognize the intimate connection between the health and wholeness of individuals and their communities. Communities torn by racism, poverty, violence, war and homelessness are not whole communities. Communities that neglect the needs of the elderly, of persons with handicapping conditions, of

Signs of brokenness: people fleeing civil strife, homes reduced to rubble, endemic poverty and unhealthy living conditions, people searching for freedom from oppression.

United Methodist Board of Global Ministries

United Methodist Board of Global Ministries

persons who are abused, of single-parent families, of children, youth and the unemployed foster brokenness, despair, alienation and sickness. Churches cannot work for the health and wholeness of individuals without addressing critical questions to those community structures which are entrusted with protecting and promoting health and wholeness.

Health for All is about theology and ethics. It is a journey toward newness of life. It is an exodus from unhealthy patterns of living. This goal puts all other priorities in proper perspective. It points to the interrelatedness of health, peace, justice, equality, education, sustaining relationships and meaningful work. It exposes all that is opposed to health at the individual, social and corporate levels.

Health for All is a challenge and an opportunity to put the gospel message into action. Like the gospel, it sets people free from bondage to unnecessary suffering and all that causes it. It challenges the church to rededicate itself to the essence of the gospel by demonstrating a preferential option for the poor and all who are oppressed.

Finally, Health for All inspires a global consciousness. It proclaims in all parts of the world that peace and justice, health and wholeness are the essence of God's kingdom. It holds up the word "health" as both a vision and a reality which can be experienced now by acting for the good of the neighbor, the community and the world—in accord with God's will.

For Christians and churches everywhere, the goal of Health for All is a call to conversion, to turn our views about health upside-down. It is a call to shape new theological interpretations of health and wholeness within the context of the gospels. It calls us to live as servants in harmonious relationships with others, with God and with the entire created order.

Being clear about what Health for All means

You don't have to go far from Metro Manila, in the Philippines, to see urban poor communities. People line up to get water. They live in houses which are overcrowded and built too close together. Passageways as narrow as catwalks run between them.

Manila's urban poor live in unsanitary conditions. There is no disposal system for human waste. Only thirty-five percent of these people are employed. The other sixty-five percent have no stable income. Children grow old before their time, working at an early age to augment meager family incomes.

These families might live close to health centers and hospitals, but they wait in long lines only to find out they can't afford the expensive prescription drugs the doctors recommend.

It is not just the urban poor who suffer. Seventy percent of the Filipino people live in rural areas where the income of the average rice farmer has fallen. These landless and near-landless farmers can't provide for even the most basic needs of their families.

Because of the nature of my work I visit many different communities. One of these is Mariveles, Bataan, the site of the first Export Processing Zone. While the overall view of the zone is nice, a few minutes walk toward the town of Mariveles reveals the gross inequalities in the living conditions of the workers. The workers receive the low pay which is the main attraction for transnational corporations to set up their industries in this country.

As I visit with these workers and see how great their suffering is I recall the ad the Central Bank in the Philippines ran in Time Magazine *on September 29, 1980. The ad encouraged U.S. companies to "let your business take root in this promising side of the world. Look to the fast-rising financial capital of Asia. The Philippines. Consider its huge potential. Highly literate, English-speaking manpower. Cheap labor rates. Abundant managerial expertise. For expatriates, low maintenence and living costs— the lowest in the region.*

"Consider significant tax incentives. Clear-cut ground rules for foreign investors. Guaranteed repatriation of profits . . . all amidst a proven and bubbling economic climate.

"Consider the Philippines. Bring your business over. Till some of the most fertile investment grounds this side of the globe."

While corporations profit, the majority of Filipino workers and their families remain poor. Seventy to eighty percent of the Philippines' population live below the poverty line. The young, especially, suffer from chronic infectious illnesses passed easily from one child to another. Seven out of ten pre-schoolers are undernourished, as is seventy percent of the population. Infant mortality accounts for twenty-five percent of all deaths. In this country of great wealth and opportunity for some, the TB rates and those for polio, schistosomiasis, whooping cough, diptheria, rabies, leprosy and blindness are among the highest in the world. Poverty . . . illness . . . and injustice go together.

—*Dr. Erlinda Senturias, Manila, Philippines.*

The churches have a long history of health work. Medical missionaries have worked on every continent. Hospitals, medical schools, nursing schools and clinics have been founded. Health workers have been trained, have unselfishly risked exposure to—and some have even died from— the illnesses and diseases that ravage the areas where they work.

Over the years, many church-sponsored health workers have become concerned that too many people who are in need of health ministries are not being reached, and that new ways must be found to address the problems that cause illness in the first place. Due partly to the influence of such visionary health workers, the international health work of the churches is going through an evolutionary change. New priorities and directions are being set.

For Dr. Senturias of the National Council of Churches in the Philippines, this means more than just moving health work beyond the walls of hospitals and into the communities. It requires a new mindset, a new identification with those who are most in need. It means transferring to the people basic knowledge about identifying and treating illnesses using effective local remedies. It means working with traditional healers, helping them develop and use their skills in community-based health work. And in addition to caring for those who are already ill, it means helping communities find ways to break the cycle of poverty and injustice which is the root cause of so much suffering and illness.

The Christian Medical Commission of the World Council of Churches in Geneva, Switzerland has been working with churches and religious groups worldwide to set new directions in church health work. At regional conferences, participants have developed a new understanding of health and wholeness as "a dynamic state of well-being of the individual and the society; of physical, mental, spiritual, economic, political and social well-being; of being in harmony with each other, with the natural environment and with God."[28]

In keeping with this vision, the goal of Health for All highlights the fact that around the world a disproportionate amount of suffering and illness result from general life conditions and their social causes. Those who strive for the goal are thus concerned about the conditions under which people live and how these can be changed to support health. This is true whether conditions are those of poverty, social injustice, stress, competition, loneliness, or of lifestyle choices which threaten health and wholeness.

The goal of Health for All invites individuals and families to see health as a responsibility of living faithfully and affirming the goodness of God's creation. It highlights the importance of people being able to shape their lives free from the burdens of avoidable illness and disease. It affirms that illness is not inevitable, and that there are things individuals and communities can do to take charge of health.

Health for All means that people can experience better ways of growing up, growing old and dying with dignity. It means that basic health services will be equally distributed throughout the population. It means that every individual and family will receive the essential services they need at a price they can afford. When Health for All is a reality, people will have a voice in the health services of their communities, and those services will be directed by local needs. Social and environmental protections will free communities from threats to health which people might otherwise not be aware of, or over which they might have little control.

The goal of Health for All recognizes that health on a large scale depends on political and economic decisions; that people and communities must be able to take greater charge of all that affects their health. A healthier world *is* possible. A better state of health is possible for every person. *Prevention, participation* and *political action* in which every individual, family, community and nation can take part, can make Health for All a reality.

3. HEALTH FOR ALL MEANS *PREVENTION*

The relentless suffering endured by millions of women, men and children around the world is a sign of brokenness in God's created order—especially when most of that suffering can be prevented.

As the twentieth century draws to a close, critical questions confront every country: Does the commitment to promote health really exist? Will conditions that cause people to suffer needlessly be corrected? How can societies assure that the poor, who suffer greater risks to their health than others, live lives free of the burdens of preventable illness? Will governments, communities and individuals each assume their rightful responsibilities and take action leading to "health promotion and disease prevention"? The words sound simple and clear-cut. In reality, their success depends on a number of factors working together. Here are four examples:

First, there must be political commitment at the local, national and international levels to make both health and peace priorities. We need a world in which nations co-exist in authentic peace: peace with justice. We need a world in which current armaments expenditures can be redirected for the nurture and development of human communities where health can flourish.

Second, people have no control over many of the factors affecting their health. Social measures are therefore required to assure affordable housing, nutritious food, a safe water supply, essential drugs, a clean environment and jobs which provide adequate income. All these are necessary if individuals and families are to overcome threats to their health.

Third, people can do many things to promote their own health and protect the health of others. This may require the personal commitment of changing ones own lifestyle and attitudes. It may require the adoption of values affirming human worth over material affluence, which foster good health habits, which work to diminish crime and violence and which oppose all forms of oppression.

Fourth, supportive communities are crucial to health promotion. Friends, families, social organizations, congregations—whatever their nature, they provide the love, care and connectedness essential to health and wholeness.

To better illustrate the complex nature of health promotion and disease prevention, three situations will be described in this chapter. They focus on health issues in North America and the third world and illustrate the many factors which, when dealt with effectively, can enable millions of people to live more abundant lives and take greater charge of their own health.

Poor in North America: An older woman's story

Sheila Bond is seventy-nine and has been widowed for thirty-five years. After her husband died, she worked as a seamstress in the clothing industry until the company went out of business seventeen years ago. No one wanted to hire her back then because of her age.

Social Security provides Mrs. Bond with $450.00 per month, which is too much to entitle her to food stamps or Medicaid. She confides that she is hungry toward the end of the month. She needs new glasses, orthopedic shoes and a hearing aid: items not covered by Medicare but essential to her ability to function on her own.

She considers herself in fairly good health for her age, though she suffers from chronic degenerative conditions. Her brown lung disease is related to twenty years of work in the textile industry. She began as a textile worker at age sixteen when there were no warnings about the effects of prolonged unprotected exposure to cotton dust. In her younger years, Mrs. Bond did not know there were things she could do to prevent her osteoporosis. She had always been told a "widow's hump" was a natural phenomenon of old age for women.

There is a church-sponsored senior center in Mrs. Bond's neighborhood which she thinks of as her second home. Her friendships there relieve her of the terrible isolation and loneliness she felt before the center opened. She is grateful for the services provided by health personnel who stop at the center to monitor blood pressure and give foot care. A course at the center on nutrition and aging has made Mrs. Bond aware of her nutritional needs. Lunch at the center provides her with a balanced main meal and helps her live within her budget. On cold winter days, the center is more comfortable than her less well-heated apartment.

Sheila Bond's story is similar to those of a growing number of older women in North America. Women constitute nearly three quarters of the aged poor today. In the United States, women in Mrs. Bond's bracket are the fastest-growing poverty group. In addition, eighty percent of elderly persons living alone are women. Like five million other women between ages forty and sixty-five today, Mrs. Bond had no health insurance after her husband died, and like eighty percent of all retirement-age women, she has no pension. Social Security is her only income. She has no savings. She is typical of many women who retire on half the income men have had. After caring for her husband for five years before he died, she continued as the unremunerated caregiver to her sister for eight years.

Asked what worries her most as she tries to maintain her health and independent living, Mrs. Bond replies, "income". For Sheila Bond, like millions of older women, a major health concern is to have adequate income to pay for food, rent, utilities and uncovered medical expenses. Mrs. Bond believes she can keep herself fairly healthy if she can make ends meet financially week by week.

Among other things, Mrs. Bond is a realist. She knows that most things affecting her financial situation—and thus her health—are outside her control. Food and utility costs, rent increases, how cold the winter will be, whether the senior center remains open, the amount of her Social Security cost-of-living increase, how governmental decisions about Medicare and Medicaid affect the care she needs—all these are factors over which she has very little power.

The health of an older woman, like the health of any person whose income is low, reflects her social conditions. Sheila Bond works hard to promote and protect her health, to maintain a healthy attitude and to do all she can to avoid illness. But health promotion depends on more than any individual can do alone.

Mrs. Bond's needs are like those of many other persons. They must be addressed if the goal of Health for All is to be a reality. Moreover, none of her needs fall outside the realm of religious concern. When one's faith is lived for and with one's neighbor, the religious response becomes a cry of protest against all that keeps people in desperate need, struggling to stay well. Faith places demands on us when we are confronted with the needs of our neighbors.

With regard to Mrs. Bond and others like her, the absolute demands laid on individuals and communities include the provision of senior centers, home delivered meals and visitation services. Beyond this there are the political, economic and social changes required to remove the burdens of poverty, insecurity and isolation faced by too many persons in their later years.

It is love for the neighbor that compels individuals to seek legislative changes giving people the opportunity to work, to work under healthy, safe conditions and to receive just compensation and benefits, whether their work is within or outside the home. It is love for the neighbor that motivates concern that people have adequate social and economic support when they are caregivers and insures that home health care will be available and affordable when needed. The gospel of love and justice demands such political and social responses as these.

Mrs. Bond is only one person, but her story is legion. She is a member of one of the fastest-growing population groups in North America: older persons. As with the vast majority of people living in industrialized countries, her main health problems are chronic and degenerative.

The infectious diseases which were rampant in North America at the turn of this century have been replaced by major chronic diseases: heart disease, cancer and stroke. Accidents and injuries also exact a fearsome toll of death and disability, particularly among the young and the elderly.

"Americans are now spending more than $1 billion a day on health care. By 1990, daily health expenditures are expected to rise to more than $2 billion. Older persons are particularly vulnerable. Their average out-of-pocket payments have risen dra-

matically, *from $698 to over $1,500 between 1970 and 1984, an increase of 122 percent. If no action is taken to stem the rise in cost, older persons will be paying a shocking 40 percent of their incomes for health care by 1995"*.[29] *Experts agree if health care costs are to be contained, which they must be, difficult decisions will have to be made to ensure that people are not denied the essential care they need.*

Today, "the concern with equity that characterized the 1960's and 1970's has given way to concern with 'cost containment', which in practice has largely come to mean reductions in social expenditures for services for those who need them most."[30] *Aware that too many older persons are being discharged from hospitals "quicker and sicker," some older-adult advocacy groups are recommending concrete steps to take to "cut the cost and keep the care."*[31] *Persons concerned about the growing number of elderly people who will require long-term care point to the need for a variety of forms of care, as well as for viable financing mechanisms. These health experts also stress the importance of disease prevention and health promotion measures.*

It was not until Mrs. Bond was in her seventies that she realized that her major health problems could have been avoided, or their risks significantly reduced. Prevention of her brown lung disease would have required a work environment designed and regulated for worker health and safety. Prevention of her osteoporosis would have required greater knowledge on the part of her physicians—and herself—about bone mass loss.

Even in her present situation, however, there are health promotion strategies which could help Mrs. Bond maintain the health she has. Some of them are, or soon might be, out of her reach. For Mrs. Bond does not live in a nation that recognizes access to health care as a "right". If she does not have money for glasses and a hearing aid, for food, adequate shelter or medications, her chances of becoming ill are increased. If she does not have outside contacts, isolation and loneliness will further affect her health. If she needs and does not have access to in-home health care, she will be forced to seek hospital or nursing home care.

How the environments in which we live affect our health

Gregg Delaney is twenty-seven years old. He is in very good health and doesn't remember ever having been really sick. Like his mother and father, who are in their early fifties, he is athletic. He and his brothers and sisters get together with their parents for two weeks every year to hike and bicycle on vacation. Gregg always took health for granted, assuming it was something that just happened. That's what he thought until 1985.

That year, his first as a news reporter, Gregg was asked to cover a number of conferences. Two stick in his mind. One was about the critical health situation of Native Americans. Not until then had he been aware that Native Americans die younger than any other racial group in the United States, with barely one-third living to age sixty-five. According to JoAnn Kauffman, a member of the Nez Perce Tribe and executive director of the Seattle Indian Health Board, "alcohol is directly related to five of the top ten killers of Indians. It is involved in seventy-five percent of all fatal accidents, eighty percent of all suicides and ninety percent of all homicides," and yet, "the Indian Health Service provides less than one percent of its annual budget for treatment or prevention of this disease."[32]

From Ms. Kauffman, Gregg learned that alcohol is wasting the lives of young Native Americans in the same way alcohol and other drugs are spoiling the hopes and health of so many North American children and youth. With regard to Native American youth and young adults, Ms. Kauffman reported that "the real waste and carnage begins at age fourteen and peaks before age forty-four. Alcohol's victims are young. Alcohol invades the quiet of our unborn. It disintegrates families and inflicts emotional, physical and sexual abuse on our young. It mutilates our teenagers and scatters their bodies across local highways and jail cells. It steals the dreams of our most gifted students, leaving them bitter and angry with a system they never had the chance to challenge."[33]

In follow-up research to learn more about the factors affecting the health of Native Americans, Gregg learned that blacks are the only population group with a higher poverty rate. The most recent census figures indicate that Native Americans living on reservations have an unemployment rate of almost twenty-eight percent—a rate nearly four times higher than that of the general U.S. population. Gregg discovered that much of the housing built by the United States government for Native Americans lacks the basic amenities that most people take for granted. Not only have twenty thousand existing homes been built without indoor toilets, another two thousand nine hundred planned for construction will also lack plumbing facilities. Gregg also learned that Native American death rates are disproportionately higher than among the general U.S. population; for tuberculosis, five hundred percent higher; for alcoholism, four hundred fifty-one percent higher; for automobile accidents, one hundred fifty-four percent higher; for youth and young adult suicide, one hundred fifty percent higher, and for pneumonia and influenza, sixty-four percent higher.[13]

In interviews with members of the American Indian Health Care Association, Gregg was reminded of the impact of a people's history on their health: "For hundreds of years American Indians have lost their culture, traditions, land, and social and economic bases due to a paternalistic government approach to Indian affairs. The relationships with the dominant white society have been those of conflict for American Indians. The conflicts have left Indians with a destruction of their societies, culture, traditions, and families. The defeats were in the forms of: language, traditions, poor societal and individual identity problems. The defeats have led to increases in disease . . ."[35]—disease which reflects itself in societal as well as personal health problems.

The second conference Gregg attended gave him a look at another slice of life in the U.S. to which he had never been exposed: the lives of women and children in Appalachia. Gregg heard women testify before the House Select Committee on Hunger that when their food stamps run out, bread and potatoes are the staple food they feed their families. Some women said their stamps always run out in mid-month because since the nearest supermarket is thirty miles away and they have no transportation to get there, they have to buy food at higher prices from stores in town. He heard other women talk about how grateful they are for small garden plots that are the main source of their families' food. A few women said they would like to have more land, but there is none available because so much of it is owned by out-of-state corporations. All of the women talked about their children's chronic colds and coughs and the fact that some of their husbands had been without work for most of the year.

Appalachia is "a paradox of poverty in the midst of plenty." That is the way Ronald Eller, director of Appalachian Studies at the University of Kentucky in Lexington, characterizes the situation of many Appalachian families. Eller cites the fact that in the Appalachian region, unemployment ranges from fifteen percent to forty-five percent on the average, and as high as seventy percent in some cases, with no hope of jobs in sight for some. He cites a rise in infant mortality due to a lack of health services. His studies indicate that many people still live without electricity or indoor plumbing and that there is widespread well water contamination in the region.[36]

After college, Gregg had served for two years with the Peace Corps in Nigeria, helping to start an adult non-formal education program. He had little awareness at the time that so many North Americans shared the same reality of hunger, poverty, inadequate housing and poor health care that he had seen among the families he had worked with in Africa.

After the conferences on the health of Native Americans and hunger in Appalachia, Gregg decided he wanted his work as a journalist to focus on health issues and the non-medical factors which directly affect the health of individuals and the communities in which they live. After completing a year-long university program on the sociology and politics of health, his perceptions about health—and all that needs to be done to protect and promote health—changed dramatically.

During that year he learned that there are four major factors contributing to disease and death. The order of their priority surprised him. For persons living in industrialized countries, behavioral factors and unhealthy lifestyles and living conditions have the greatest effect on health. One's environment is the second most important factor and is being recognized as playing an increasingly larger role. Human biological factors play the third most significant role. Inadequacies in the health care system are the fourth factor.

Gregg's professor reminded the class that illness is usually not a random event striking this or that person by chance. In fact, individuals and their communities can have greater influence over health than they realize. But in order for people to have more control, the many environments in which they function must become more health-promoting and health-protecting. And the changes that are required can only be brought about by concerted action on the part of individuals, families, communities and the governments responsible to them.

Evidence is increasing that the onset of ill health is strongly linked to one's physical, social, economic and family environments.

Influences in the physical environment may include: contamination of air, water, and food; workplace hazards; radiation exposure; excessive noise; dangerous consumer products; and unsafe highway design. Over the past one hundred years our physical environment has markedly altered. Many changes reflect important progress, but they bring new health hazards—among them, thousands of synthetic chemicals (with new ones being introduced at an annual rate of about one thousand) and the by-products of transportation, manufacturing, agriculture and energy production.

The major factors in the socio-economic environment which affect health are income level, housing, and employment status. Persons who are poor face more and different health risks than people in higher income groups: inadequate medical care with too few preventive services; a more hazardous physical environment; greater stress; less education; greater unemployment or job frustration; and income inadequate for good nutrition, safe housing and other basic needs.

Family relationships also constitute an important environmental component for health. Drastic alterations may occur in family circumstances as spouses die or separate, as children leave home or an elderly parent moves in.

An abrupt change in social dynamics can create emotional stress severe enough to trigger serious physical illness or even death. On the other hand, loving family support can contribute to mental and physical well-being and provide a stable atmosphere within which children can develop in a healthy manner.[37]

31

Gregg also learned that the increase in the United States total health care spending from $41 billion in 1965 to over $400 billion in 1985 did not yield the gains that had been expected. In part, this was because the expenditures were directed to the treatment rather than to the prevention of disease. "If we consider the health of entire populations and the health of society in general, medical interventions have had very little impact or effect. By and large, the improved life expectancy at birth for Americans over the past one hundred years can be credited primarily to activities that include environmental improvements, safe housing and water supplies, waste disposal, regulations in food safety and immunization programs. . . . Just one of these simple prevention and promotion measures probably has more influence on our health than all the hospital beds in the United States."[38]

Health for All means disease prevention and health promotion, but look where the money goes.[39]

Of every dollar America spends for health, 97 cents pays for treatment, 2.5 cents helps prevent disease and a half-penny is spent teaching people how to stay healthy.

Of every dollar the United States spends for health, 97 cents pays for treatment, 2.5 cents helps prevent disease and half a penny is spent teaching people how to stay healthy.

Gregg's courses on the sociology of health enabled him to examine how habits which destroy health are often socially reinforced and powerfully condoned by the media. Cigarette use is a prime example. In the United States, one thousand persons die each day from problems related to cigarette smoking. In 1985, lung cancer surpassed breast cancer as the leading cause of death by cancer among U.S. women. According to the director of the National Institute on Drug Abuse, smoking cigarettes made of tobacco is the top U.S. drug problem in terms of personal health.

Excessive cigarette advertising clearly nullifies the impact of warnings that cigarettes are dangerous to health. And as the number of male smokers has declined, cigarette ads have taken an insidious turn, targeting women as their major market group.

Gregg's professor reminded the class that the protection of free market enterprise has been a hallmark of the United States economy. He then asked, "What happens to a nation's concern for health promotion and disease prevention when a product known to be the single most important preventable cause of death in a nation continues to be manufactured, advertised and sold purely for profit?"

In a course on health maintenance, Gregg learned that seven of the ten leading causes of death in the U.S. today could be substantially reduced if persons at risk paid attention to five habits: diet, smoking, rest, lack of exercise and substance abuse. He completed the course recognizing the significant role of personal behavior in promoting or endangering health. But he also learned that not all behavior is within the power of the individual to control, for instance:

• A person might know what foods are best to eat, but one's food options might be limited. Too many people who live on inadequate incomes run low on food money during the third week of the month. Others who may or may not know the importance of good nutrition consume whatever foods they prefer, although these may well increase their risks of disease.

• A single mother might need to work two jobs. In her sixteen-hour work day there is little time for rest and no one to help her raise her child or keep house. She knows she is neglecting her health through overwork. But without the second job she cannot afford day care for her child.

• Young persons in their most impressionable years must make personal lifestyle choices in the context of a society which considers drinking, smoking and violent behavior glamorous and equates who you are with what you own. The hopes and dreams of thousands of youth today are frustrated by unemployment and inadequate education—and they turn to the use of drugs. Far more young Americans die between the ages of fifteen and twenty-four than was true twenty years ago. Seventy-five percent of these premature deaths are from accidents, homicides and suicides. Violence, injury, alcohol and drug abuse, unwanted pregnancies and sexually-transmitted diseases are the most common health problems of these youth and young adults. Though chronic diseases are not among the major causes of death for this group, lifestyle patterns formed during these years influence later susceptability to heart disease, stroke, cancer, cirrhosis of the liver and hypertension. The characteristics which can lead to these diseases can begin as early as childhood. Today, as many as forty percent of American children in the age group eleven to fourteen are estimated to have one or more of the risk factors associated with heart disease: overweight, high blood pressure, high blood cholesterol, cigarette smoking, lack of exercise or diabetes.[40]

• Nearly every month there are news reports about chemical wastes which have not been properly disposed of or stored. Too frequently, the families in these areas have been unaware of this potential threat to their health. Several thousand disposal sites similar to the one discovered at Love Canal exist across the United States. Some of these sites contain large quantities of unknown chemicals, including highly toxic materials which can contaminate surface or ground water supplies as well as the atmosphere itself. In addition, "about eighty percent of Americans now live in urban areas where toxic gases or particulate matter pollute the air. Most of the pollution results from combustion of fossil fuels by automobiles and in industrial activities."[41]

• People also face risks from exposure to dangerous chemicals in the workplace. "Despite risks of serious disease or injury, most workers are unprotected. Worksite exposure standards have been established for only a few toxic substances. Perhaps twenty percent of all cancers may be related to carcinogens encountered in the workplace."[42]

• Migrant workers and seasonal crop-pickers are among the high-risk groups suffering from sub-standard working and living conditions. "The underlying conditions that contribute to the poor physical and mental health of migrants and other hired seasonal farmworkers have changed little over the years. Housing continues to be dilapidated and overcrowded. Water supplies continue to be inadequate and subject to contamination in many places. Flies continue to swarm over people, food and mounds of garbage. Rats continue to breed in trash-strewn premises. Most worksites continue to lack even such amenities as toilets and handwashing facilities. . . [and] toxic substances may be in frequent use for pest control."[43]

Reflecting on this situation, Helen Johnson, author of *Health for the Nation's Harvesters,* writes: "So long as these living and working conditions continue, babies will be stricken and some will die of diarrheal disease and other preventable conditions. Hungry children will fail to develop minds and bodies at a normal rate. Women will be at 'high risk' for maternity care. Preventable illnesses and disability will afflict workers"[44] and their families.

• Attempts on the part of the government to summarily remove benefits from large numbers of disabled persons in order to decrease government spending have a direct effect on the ability of many such persons to protect and promote their own health.

All of these considerations helped Gregg make the connection between personal behavior and social factors which influence health. It was easy to see the connection between illnesses and one's lifestyle. But in health promotion and disease prevention, a delicate balance exists between what individuals can do for themselves and the social protections and services that are needed to guard their health.

"There is no need for us to fall into the trap of choosing whether health is mainly our personal and individual responsibility or mainly a responsibility of society, for this is an over-simplification. It is true that the leading causes of death and disability include disorders in which choice plays a part, such as alcoholism, obesity, accidents and certain disorders of stress. But. . . it

would be shortsighted if we overemphasized the role of the individual in the promotion of his or her own health, important as it is, and neglected to look at the role of society in bringing about and perpetuating conditions that interfere with health, place people at greater risk of disease or produce growth-interfering conditions. As important as it is that we, as individuals, stop smoking; drink moderately, if at all; eat a nourishing, well-balanced diet; exercise regularly and have adequate sleep, it is equally important that individuals learn how to deal constructively with and to alter the negative, destructive aspects of society." [45]

The child-survival revolution: Addressing one of the most obvious signs of brokenness in God's created order

Children cannot put into words the nature of their injury when their needs are not the priority of their communities, their nation or the world, or when they are deprived of things their parents cannot or do not know how to provide. Yet the cry that pierces the night uttered from the throat of a sick child is eloquent and specific. Crying is the only language a child's pain knows. For a majority of the world's children, crying is about hunger and pain and strength that is seeping away. The child's scream is about unanswered need: the injury done when the keepers of nations entrust the future to something other than the healthy growth of today's children, who are the world's only tomorrow.

Chilean Nobel prizewinning poet Gabriela Mistral writes:

We are guilty of many errors and faults, but our worst crime is
    abandoning the children, neglecting the fountain of life.
Many of the things we need can wait.
The child cannot.
Right now is the time his bones are being formed, his blood is being
    made and his senses are being developed.
To him we cannot answer, "Tomorrow"
His name is "Today". [46]

In the developing countries of the world, forty thousand children die needlessly each day from preventable diseases and illnesses. At least twenty thousand of these lives could be saved every day—and several million additional children annually could be spared physical and mental disability—through simple, basic health-promotion methods.

Breastfeeding, growth monitoring, oral rehydration therapy and immunizations form the backbone of a child-survival revolution which can bring inestimable hope to parents and children living in rural poverty, in barrios, shanty towns, bantustans, and in tenement houses in cities large and small around the world.

The child's plaintive scream is about unanswered need: the harm done when the keepers of the nations entrust the future to something other than the healthy growth and development of today's children, who are the world's only tomorrow.

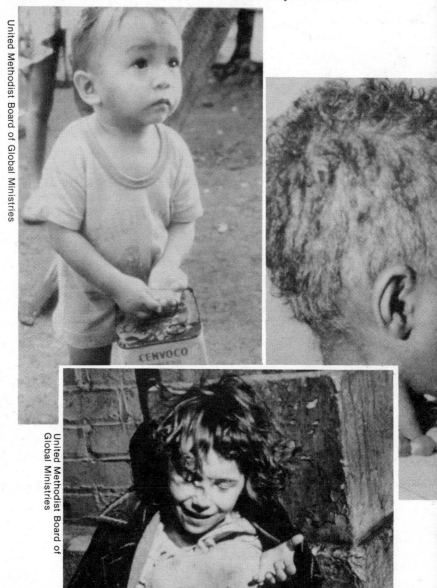

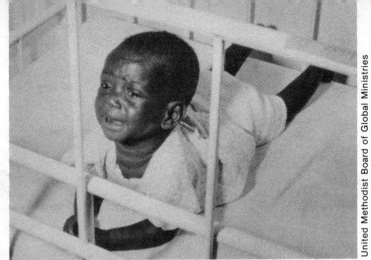

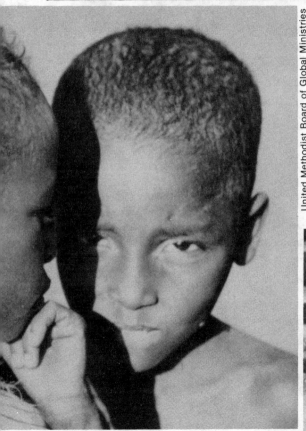

Today's children: the world's future

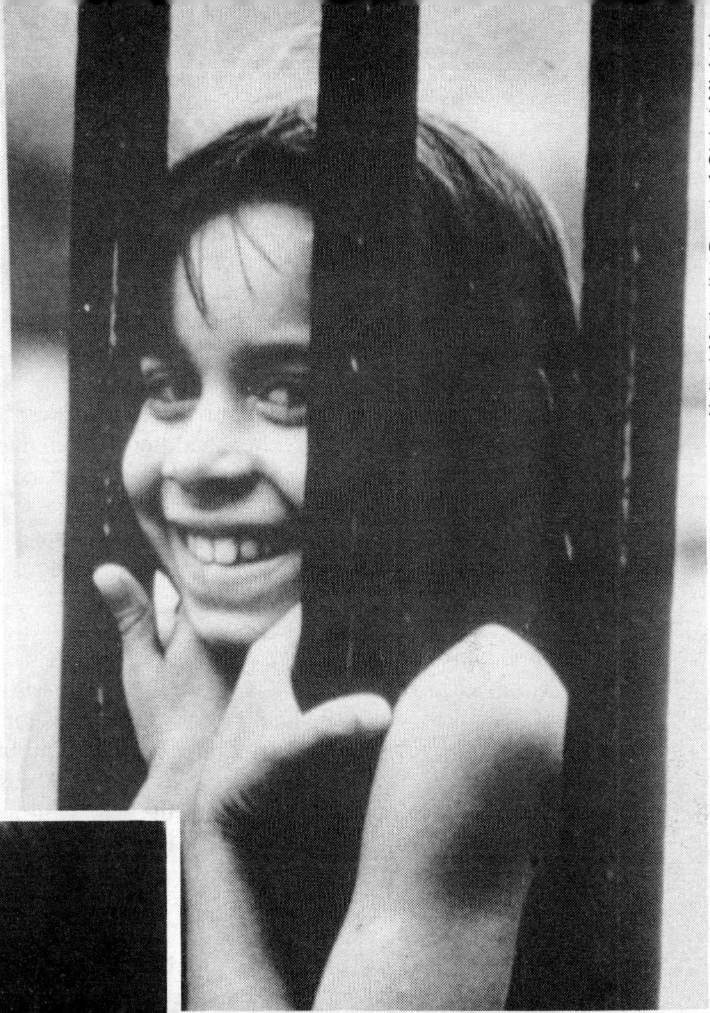

United Methodist Board of Global Ministries

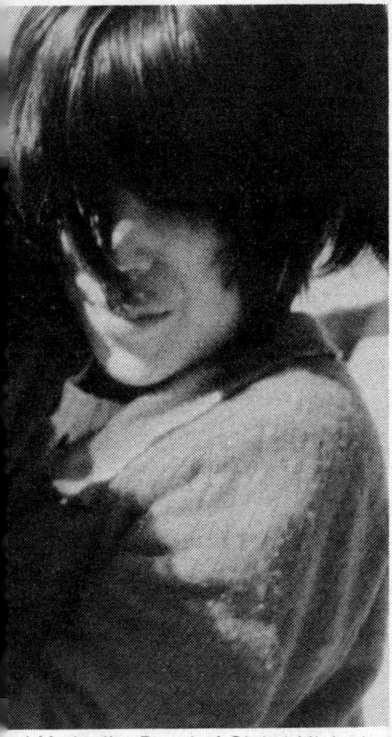

ed Methodist Board of Global Ministries

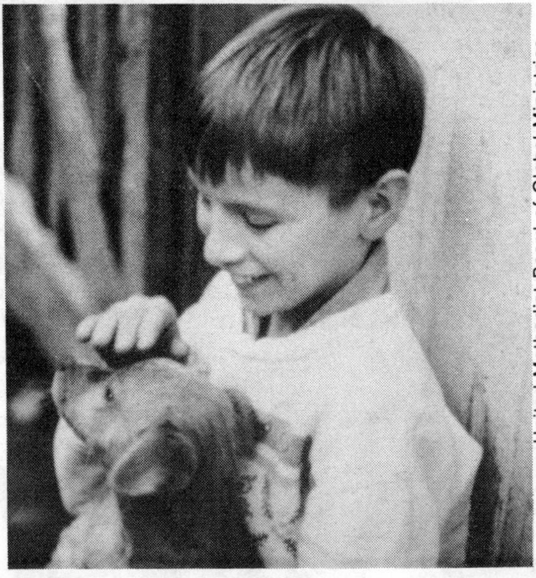

United Methodist Board of Global Ministries

FOUR BASIC METHODS FOR SAVING CHILDREN'S LIVES

(1) *Breast-feeding and healthy weaning practices*

In all countries, including the United States and Canada, breastfeeding is again being encouraged over the use of breastmilk substitutes. In many parts of the world, the return to breastfeeding has involved widespread campaigns to re-educate women and health professionals that "the breast is best"; and to counter the multi-million dollar advertising of corporations which have sought larger markets and higher profits through the sale of infant products.

Breastfeeding provides sufficient nourishment for most infants until four to six months of age. Thereafter, additional foods are needed to complement breastfeeding and assure that infants receive the protein and other nutrients necessary for normal growth. Improving weaning practices and the development of low-cost, nutritious weaning foods in the home is a central aspect of child development, in addition to breastfeeding.

(2) *Growth monitoring*

Only about one percent of the world's children are visibly and obviously malnourished. But more than a quarter of the developing world's children suffer from invisible malnutrition. Making the problem of malnutrition visible to the mother is one of the simplest and most important of all methods for protecting and promoting the healthy growth of many millions of infants during their vulnerable early years. Growth monitoring is an essential aid to child health regardless of where the child lives. The growth of the human brain takes place largely before birth and during the first two years of a child's life. Invisible malnutrition—prolonged, undetected and untreated—can have a marked affect on a child's overall health and mental development. In addition, invisible malnutrition will often result in a child conserving his or her energy by not engaging in activities with other children—activities which help children learn how to interact with others in their environment.

(3) *Oral rehydration therapy*

Diarrhea is a major cause of death among children in some parts of the world. Today, families everywhere can be taught a basic method to prevent diarrhea-related deaths. This involves the use of oral rehydration therapy to treat diarrhea-induced dehydration, using homemade solutions of water and small amounts of sugar and salt. Through this method, families can take charge of a major child health problem and prevent the needless deaths of five million children each year.

(4) *Immunization*

Every six seconds in the developing world, a child dies and another is disabled by a disease which can be prevented by immunization. The

Breastfeeding and immunizations are saving children's lives.

Peter Magubane

WHO, Geneva

six major communicable diseases of childhood—measles, whooping cough, tetanus, polio, diphtheria and tuberculosis—can be eliminated. Immunization against these diseases costs approximately five dollars per child. Raising and allocating funds to insure the immunization of children is a priority of the child-survival revolution.[47]

FOUR ADDITIONAL HEALTH-PROMOTION STEPS TOWARD IMPROVING THE HEALTH OF MOTHERS, CHILDREN AND FAMILIES

In addition to the four basic methods cited above, the child-survival revolution recognizes four additional health promotion steps which are more difficult and costly to implement. Nonetheless, their importance is obvious and critical. Three of these have to do with improvements in the lives of women.

(1) *Family spacing and maternal and child care*

It is estimated that another five million children's deaths could be prevented each year through programs to give women more choice over both family size and child spacing. Whatever the country, too many births occuring too soon after the previous birth negatively affects the health of the mother, the developing baby and the other children in the family. Associated with this is every women's need for adequate care during and after pregnancy, and for a person trained in childbirth to assist her during delivery. Statistics from the Indian subcontinent make somber reading: ". . . in Pakistan, maternal deaths in *one month* are equal to the maternal deaths in *one year* in North America, Europe, Australia and Japan combined."[48] Out of every twenty Pakistani women who become pregnant, one dies; and in parts of India, one in every fifty pregnancies ends in the death of the mother.[49]

(2) *Food supplements*

Another step that helps save infant lives involves the provision of food supplements to women who otherwise would be inadequately nourished before and during pregnancy. This addresses one of the least-known but most important reasons for infant deaths in both North America and developing countries: low birthweight babies. Many babies are undernourished in the womb largely because the mother herself is undernourished. Food supplements reduce the risk of low birthweight and build up a woman's own health and energy. Food supplements are often continued after birth to maintain the woman's food energy store. Appropriate weaning foods for the child are also considered food supplements.

In North America, educational programs to prevent low birthweight babies stress the need for adequate prenatal care, including medical care, nutritional services and social support, and encourage women not to drink alcohol, use illicit drugs or smoke during pregnancy because of the effect these habits have on their own health and on the growth and development of the fetus.

Child health campaigns in the United States emphasize that "low birthweight babies are twenty times more likely to die than babies born at a normal birthweight. Two-thirds of all low birthweight infants will require extended hospital care during the first year of life at an average of $1,000 per day. One in four low birthweight infants will be left permanently disabled by conditions such as retardation, cerebral palsy, vision and hearing disabilities."[50]

(3) Female education

For almost every child, the mother is the most important health care provider. The level of the mother's education is a key determinant of her child's health. The education—and subsequent empowerment—of women can have a revolutionary impact on the well-being of children and the size of the family.

(4) Increasing family incomes

High infant mortality rates are heavily associated with the inadequate income of poorer families in both the industrialized countries and the third world. This is graphically illustrated in the following chart based on a study in New Delhi, India.

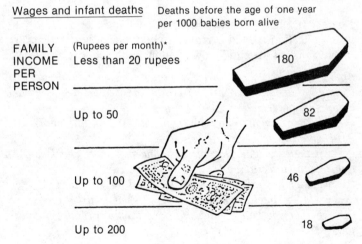

Wages and infant deaths — Deaths before the age of one year per 1000 babies born alive

FAMILY INCOME PER PERSON (Rupees per month)*	
Less than 20 rupees	180
Up to 50	82
Up to 100	46
Up to 200	18

Figures based on a study in New Delhi, India.
*1 $ US = 10 rupees

Note that when per capita income increased from twenty rupees (two dollars) to two hundred rupees (twenty dollars) per month, infant deaths dropped from one hundred eighty per one thousand babies born alive to eighteen. Poverty may not be a disease, but it is an overwhelmingly large factor in the persistently high rates of infant suffering and death.

"In a poor community in the developing world. . . a child is likely to be ill for sixteen to twenty weeks (four to five months) of a year. In one study of children in an extremely poor area of Bangladesh, young children were found to be ill for three-quarters of their lives."[51]

The challenge of a child-survival revolution is a challenge for both governments and people. "Children cannot start such a revolution in their own defense. Yet in the last year alone, the fifteen million young children who have died in the developing world is the equivalent of the entire under-five population of the United States of America. On a European scale, it is as if the combined under-five population of Britain, France, Italy, Spain and the Federal Republic of Germany had been wiped out in a year. And for every child who has died, another has been left blind or deaf or crippled or retarded."[52] Most of these fifteen million deaths are the result of shamefully simple and ordinary causes.

Saving the lives of twenty thousand children a day will not happen just because of the existence of the elements above. Rather, parents everywhere must be "empowered with new knowledge about child protection—and supported from all sides in the task of putting that knowledge into practice."[53] More than any one thing, child survival depends on the creation of a new ethic of health care itself.

"Doctors and hospitals cannot create anything like as strong a wall of basic protection around a growing child as can be provided by the informed action of the child's own parents in the child's own home."[54]

Almost all of the most powerful methods now available for protecting children's lives are based on knowledge, decisions and actions by parents:
  • *whether a woman has a little more rest or a little more food in pregnancy;*
  • *whether she goes for at least one pre-natal check and an anti-tetanus injection;*
  • *whether her infant is breast-fed, and for how long;*
  • *when she begins weaning, and with what mix of foods;*
  • *whether she knows how and how often to prepare a child's food;*
  • *whether she pays particular attention to a child's feeding during and after an illness;*
  • *whether parents make up and use oral rehydration solutions during episodes of diarrhea;*
  • *whether parents check the child's weight gain regularly;*
  • *whether they take a child on three separate occasions to be immunized;*
  • *how they decide whether or when to have another child.*

These are all decisions which have far more effect on whether a child lives or dies, whether a child grows normally or is stunted, than anything a doctor or a hospital can do. And whatever other influences are at play, these are all decisions that are taken and acted on by the family itself.

The child-survival revolution is part of a much wider shift in thinking about health care. Worldwide, it is now becoming clear that the next generation of advances in human health will come not through greater dependence on medical services but through the return of primary responsibility and resources for health to the individual, the family and the community.[55]

DISEASE PREVENTION AND REHABILITATION

These are the dual concerns of the child-survival revolution. Millions of children suffer the disabling effects of preventable injuries, illnesses and poor nutrition. This is particularly true in the developing countries where more than one hundred million children with disabilities live—countries where as many as one out of every twenty or thirty children may be severely affected.

The Christian Medical Commission emphasizes the need for community-based primary health care programs to work with families to reduce the disabling effects of blindness, deafness, neurological impairments and mobility difficulties.

Too frequently, the most disabling factors affecting the lives of persons with disabilities are societal attitudes that render them dependent, hidden away or on the margin of society. Families, health workers and communities need to develop positive attitudes about the abilities of persons with disabilities—this should be a major objective of local health and rehabilitation work. Persons with disabilities can take part in and contribute to the life of their communities if practical, affordable methods are developed to enable them to do so.

As persons with disabilities become leaders in community health work, they set an example of what health and wholeness are about. Out of his long experience in village health care, David Werner writes: "physically disabled young people often make exceptional community health workers. Many . . . have developed an exceptional 'view of the world'. They feel a sort of brother-and-sisterhood with other . . . exploited and oppressed peoples. They are committed to working in their own different ways toward a fairer world—one in which the silent speak out and the weak grow strong by joining hands."[56]

The wide-scale success of the child-survival revolution will depend heavily on new approaches to health promotion, rehabilitation and socio-economic development designed to benefit individuals, families and communities. These approaches will need the full support of local and national governments committed to health priorities and budgets which address the most basic health needs of the majority of the population.

What difference can simple rehabilitation at the village level make...

...to the disabled child?
...to the child's family?
...to the community?

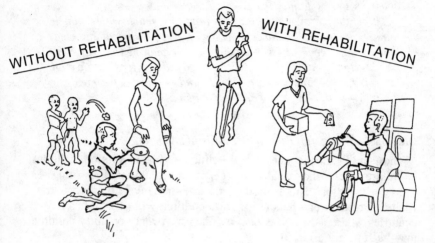

WITHOUT REHABILITATION

WITH REHABILITATION

Credit: *Contact*

Community-based primary health care is one approach which has proven successful in promoting health, preventing disease and improving family incomes. One such program, which has been of inestimable importance to the health of children, their families and communities is highlighted in the next chapter, which emphasizes that Health for All means *participation*.

The child-survival revolution isn't just about health promotion in developing countries, though some of the most glaring statistics about poor health come from those vast regions of the world. Child health promotion has to do with North America as well—with everywhere children are born and grow up.

In the United States, child health concerns include the following issues:

• the U.S. infant mortality rate is higher than it is in at least fifteen other countries and is declining more slowly than in most of those other nations;
• low birthweight is a principal factor in neonatal and infant mortality and can lead to numerous health and developmental problems in children who survive. Two-thirds of all newborns who die were low birthweight babies;
• pregnancy at too young an age puts both mother and child at risk. Early pregnancy frequently means the end of a girl's opportunity for education and advancement;

- poor nutrition, cigarette smoking and the use of alcohol and other substances during pregnancy have a marked effect on the developing child and are detrimental to maternal health as well;
- though infant mortality among whites continues to decrease, infant mortality among blacks and non-white Hispanics remains disproportionately high;
- too many women who need prenatal care are not receiving it; thirty-eight percent of black women do not receive care during the first three months of pregnancy;
- increasing numbers of children are being raised in poverty, further impeding access to adequate health services and living conditions which promote health;
- because access to needed health care is not a "right" in the U.S., some clinics, hospitals and physicians require uninsured women to pay money in advance of care—money which poor women frequently do not have;
- many women and children in the U.S. also need food supplements. Some of these women depend heavily on food stamps and Supplemental Feeding Programs for Women, Infants, and Children. Levels of funding and eligibility requirements for these programs can directly affect the health and well-being of women and their children;
- nurse midwives can provide quality care to pregnant women; some women prefer their services over those of physicians. Laws and regulations affecting the practice of nurse midwives affect the kind of care women can receive;
- when maternal and child-care funds decrease, clinics close, further limiting women's access to affordable care;
- the public remains divided over whether or how teenagers should have access to sex education and contraception;
- physical, mental and sexual abuse of children affect the health of children and families alike.

These concerns illustrate problems within the U.S. which must be addressed by individuals, communities and government if health promotion and disease prevention are to be realities. Many of them are related to deep-seated social problems of poverty and racism which have an undeniable impact on people's state of health and their access to health care and to living conditions which promote health.

The gospel has a clear message concerning the importance of the millions of child lives lost each year throughout the world. Its words are far different from the message children and their parents receive in a society of competing values and priorities in which, if they are poor, they assume a lowly place.

Against the present reality of children's needless suffering and death, the gospel upholds the magnitude of hope and the fullness of life for children. Its forceful words echo the message that children are infinitely precious, that they have a pre-eminent place in the Kingdom of God here and now.

The gospel is consistent on the worth of children, on the value of becoming like children, on the need to humble oneself like a child. It also cautions against anything that would cause a child to stumble. The gospel warns against the despair and oppression that confront millions of families, against persistent forms of social neglect that can make people stumble in their faith that God is a loving God.

Our faith is in the God who sides with the poor and all who are in need, who directs and redirects human societies in the ways of peace, justice and mercy for all. To heed the gospel's warning to do nothing that would cause a child to stumble means taking sides against all that inhibits family health, development and security. It means seeing the family as a social unit with material needs and rights. It means recognizing the connection between child health and family health, between child deaths and family income; between improvements in the lives of women and smaller, healthier families. It means taking concrete action to ensure that families and communities are able to take charge of health. The results will be sure to improve the health of the society as a whole.

4. HEALTH FOR ALL MEANS *PARTICIPATION*

When one speaks of the goal of Health for All with regard to the developing countries of the world, the word "all" refers to massive populations. The majority of these individuals and their families have never been affected by conventional medical care that focuses more on the treatment of disease than on its prevention.

The major diseases in third world countries are preventable. They fall into two basic categories: infectious disease and those directly associated with malnutrition. The causes of most of these illnesses remain deeply rooted in the environments—physical, economic, social, cultural and political—in which people live.

The goal of Health for All does not envision health as a "product", as something hospitals and physicians "sell" and people can "buy". Nor does it see knowledge and decisions about health as something physicians and other health professionals are to control.

Health is made or broken in the environment in which a person lives—in his or her own community, his or her own home, where she or he works, where she or he is born and grows up. Promoting and maintaining health has to do with adequate, nutritious food; clean water and sanitation; healthy living conditions; adequate housing; a clean, safe environment; and adequate family income and education. It includes people's involvement in identifying their own health problems. It means they participate in finding solutions. It depends on women and girls having opportunities and status equal to that of men and boys. It means people know how to take care of their health. It requires that community services, including basic health care and health education, are available to all at a price everyone can afford—and that these services are scientifically sound, culturally acceptable and address the local needs identified by the people.

Promoting and maintaining health depends on government support of health promotion and disease prevention strategies which can reach the underserved majority, even if this means redirecting current resources or increasing health budgets.

In a growing number of countries, hospital-based care has become a luxury which people can no longer afford. This is especially true in developing countries where less than twenty percent of the population has access to hospital care. Even when such care is available, it is largely used to treat people after they become ill. Hospitals anywhere cost a lot of money to build, operate and maintain, compared with the small number of persons they serve. In some developing countries, as much as eighty percent of the national health budget is spent on serving twenty percent of the population.

Though hospital-based curative care will always be needed because not all diseases and injuries can be eliminated, such care will continue to have a small role to play in protecting and promoting people's health.

The goal of Health for All, like the child-survival revolution, depends on new approaches to health, such as community-based primary health care, which combines health promotion and disease prevention with basic treatment. Primary health care emphasizes the importance of all groups in society—farmers, educators, bankers, religious groups, women's organizations, government officials—working together to promote socio-economic and human development.

If there is a key word that describes the primary health care approach, it is "participation". One fine example of this is seen in Jamkhed, India.

Jamkhed, India: A cradle of hope and Health for All

Liberation and participation are simultaneous processes. In the words of theologian Letty Russell, "liberation is a journey with others, for others, toward God's future." In one of the poorest regions of India, hundreds of thousands of Indians are participating in activities that are liberating them from injustices and deprivations which have affected their health for generations. In a brief seventeen years, Jamkhed has become an example of the essential role of participation in the health of individuals and their communities.

It is a twelve-hour ride by jeep from Bombay to the village of Jamkhed in India's Maharashtra State. The overwhelming majority of Indians (eighty percent) live in villages similar to Jamkhed across India's vast countryside, where mere survival can be a cruel test of human ingenuity and the will to live.

In 1970, Jamkhed bore the deep scars of illness and denied justice: high rates of maternal and infant deaths; low numbers of children surviving to age five; widespread disease; the waste of human life potential; poverty and underdevelopment. What has happened in Jamkhed is the result of successful attempts to help village people take control of those factors which so dramatically affect health. Jamkhed today is a cradle of hope where the goal of Health for All is being realized and is reshaping the lives of individuals and communities.

Jamkhed's Comprehensive Rural Health Project, which serves an area of three hundred thousand people in two hundred villages, had its simple beginning in the abandoned sheds of a veterinary dispensary, with light provided by a paraffin lamp. Two Christian health workers, Mabelle and Raj Arole, began their work there among rural country people. Having received medical degrees from Vellore Christian Medical College in India and public health education at Johns Hopkins University in the United States, the Aroles were well acquainted with illnesses and how to treat them. But it was not their remarkable ability to diagnose and treat illnesses that made the difference. Suffering always wears a human face. And in the eyes of the people who came to them the Aroles saw suffering that did not have to exist. In theological terms, the health work they started in Jamkhed was intended to help people set themselves free from bondage to unnecessary suffering.

The project's primary concern is with health. Its object is to help communities do all they can to keep people from becoming ill in the first place. Its philosophy is clear: Illness and disease are not inevitable; most health problems in rural areas are easy to treat and prevent; people can learn to identify their own health problems and to develop effective solutions.

The story of Jamkhed is the story of the people themselves. These include village health workers, women's clubs, farmers' clubs, and the hundreds of thousands of individuals and families who have adopted healthier ways of living. Within Jamkhed and in neighboring villages, communal decisions are being made which promote health. People's attitudes about health are changing. Harmful cultural traditions and superstitions are being abandoned. A simple health referral system enables village people to be the key health agents. All of this has accomplished what medicines, doctors and hospitals have not been not able to do. The reason is simple: Health has very little to do with hospital-based medical care. It has to do with the intricacies of community life, with human relationships, values, power structures and concern for those most in need.

One important aspect of the health work in Jamkhed involves village-level health education and services. Today, nearly two hundred village health workers have been trained as the primary health agents of the Comprehensive Rural Health Project. Each worker is selected by the people of her particular village. Most of the women are semi-literate or illiterate; all are married and have had children. They have the sensitivity to recognize other people's needs, the patience to promote health knowledge and the compassion to care gently for the sick.

A village health worker, who sees from fifteen to twenty people a day, ensures that minor ailments do not become serious medical problems. The entire village is covered by the health worker each week; the health of each family is observed. A close bond is formed between the village women and the health worker, who cares for expectant and nursing mothers, performs deliveries and helps families time and space the birth of their children.

When the village health worker identifies problems more serious than she can treat, she seeks appropriate care through the village health referral system, which includes a mobile health clinic with a health team that visits each village once or twice a month. A thirty-bed hospital is available at the project's main center in Jamkhed, with four sub-units in selected villages. Most health work, however, is performed by the village health worker; her skills are sufficient to treat seventy-five percent of the problems in the villages.

In Jamkhed, the health care system is organized around the village health worker. If such a system of care did not exist, the majority of the people would be deprived of the community-centered activities that have made Jamkhed a cradle of hope.

The integration of health promotion, disease prevention and socio-economic development has made a difference in Jamkhed:
- *the number of women who avail themselves of prenatal care has risen from .5 percent to 80 percent;*
- *village health workers and nurses are available to help all women in childbirth;*
- *75–85 percent of families are using family-planning services to space and limit the number of children;*
- *healthier women are giving birth to healthier babies who are surviving through better care, more adequate nutrition and immunizations;*
- *in some villages, infant mortality has been reduced from 150 deaths to 18 deaths per 1,000 live births;*
- *because women have learned to give oral rehydration therapy, hospital admission for childhood diarrhea is rare;*
- *through effective childhood immunization, whooping cough, diptheria and polio have been eliminated from the project region;*
- *through nutrition education and agricultural development, malnutrition has been reduced from 30 to 8 percent;*
- *the rate of female literacy has increased and family incomes have improved;*
- *the status of women and girls has improved;*
- *villages enjoy clean water and improved sanitation;*
- *reforestation is taking place and land is being saved from soil erosion;*
- *human living areas are separated from those of goats, cattle and other animals.*

Because health does not exist in a vacuum, community groups work cooperatively with the health worker, giving attention to socio-economic development, education and other non-medical factors affecting health. The supportive efforts of the village health worker and the village clubs assure the project's all-encompassing approach to health and development.

Women's clubs, for instance, can improve the social condition of women and their children and address one of the greatest injustices found in India today: the low status of women. Through these clubs, women begin to achieve their individual and collective potential and work together to bring about change. These clubs not only help their

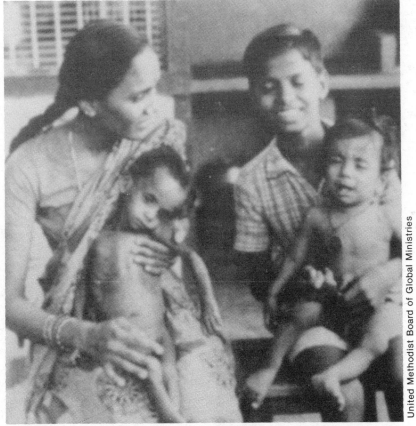

Look what can happen when boys are valued more than girls. Two-year-old twins: a girl and a boy. The boy was nursed and fed until full; his sister got what was left. In Jamkhed, women's clubs are working to see that Health for All begins in the cradle: that girl babies and boy babies are treated equally.

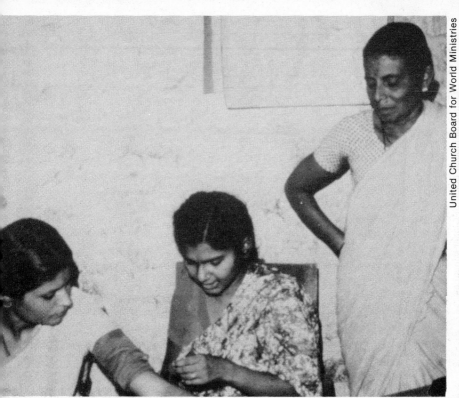

Dr. Mabelle Arole (center), Jamkhed, India

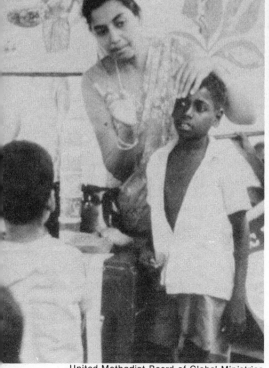

The people of Jamkhed: where Health for All means participation

members see the connection between low status and poor health, but introduce educational programs and socio-economic improvements that can break that vicious cycle. The educational programs provide basic literacy skills and teach methods of promoting child and family health. Such non-formal education, through which women recognize their inherent potential and gain an appreciation of themselves and each other, is an important link in the process of full human development. Heightened self-respect also has a direct bearing on health and well-being.

Women's clubs also promote social and economic development by helping women secure bank loans for agricultural and business enterprises. When a woman moves out of the subsistence level into economically-productive work, her family's health and well-being are affected as much as her own.

Farmers' clubs function at the village level close to the ebb and flow of daily life. Members of such clubs work together to improve food supplies and irrigation systems and to save valuable soil from erosion. Their activities contribute to the health of the entire community by focusing on clean water and improved sanitation and housing. The Comprehensive Rural Health Project encourages village men to channel their energies and hopes into programs that will benefit the entire community, especially those who are poor.

Why is the Comprehensive Rural Health Project in Jamkhed important to Christians who live in industrialized countries and who are concerned about Health for All? For one thing, Jamkhed offers a glimpse of the dynamic nature of health—the fact that health is influenced by what is mundane in life, and is dependent on the capacity of people to work together to transform their communities.

The villages of the Jamkhed program have much in common with certain urban and rural situations in North America. No matter where one lives, health is shaped by a combination of factors: by access to community-based health services that respond to local needs; by relationships based on love and compassion; by the possibility of socio-economic development for everyone in the community; by values based on commitment to justice and health; by people's respect for the natural environment; by people's taking responsibility for their own health and for protecting the health of others; by governments' actions for the good of all; by people of faith in dynamic relationship with God; by whatever opportunities and communities are created to enable people to achieve their full potential for health and wholeness.

In Jamkhed, at least seven types of health-promoting participatory behavior can be identified. The following examples point to the levels at which individuals and groups everywhere can take responsibility for health. They illustrate above all the importance of cooperative relationships which affirm the inherent dignity and rights of all persons; which break down long-standing barriers and bring reconciliation; which provide the love and acceptance which is integral to health and wholeness; which yield power to people rather than over people; which emphasize harmony with the natural environment so it can be protected and enhanced as a source of food, safe water and development. Beyond the village itself, cooperative relationships established with banks and provincial and state governments can also provide people with much-needed resources.

Types of health-promoting participatory behavior and activities in Jamkhed

(1) The most basic health-promoting behavior is that of individuals who have adopted healthier ways of living and supported changes which have improved the health of all. Thousands of people are avoiding simple illnesses and injuries by participating in classes about self-care and adequate nutrition, household cleanliness and safety, how to keep water supplies clean. At the same time, women are joining together to address alcoholism and physical abuse as serious health concerns.

(2) The families of Jamkhed are gaining new skills in caregiving that involve the whole family. Women are taking advantage of maternal and child health education. With the assistance of the village health worker, mothers are learning how to monitor children's development through the use of child growth charts; learning how to administer oral rehydration therapy to protect against diarrheal diseases; learning how and when to wean their children with locally available, nutritious weaning food; availing themselves of care before and after delivery because they know their health affects the health of their babies and the rest of the family. Children are learning how to care for the simple illnesses of their brothers and sisters. Mothers and fathers are participating in village-level immunization programs to protect their children from the six communicable diseases of childhood.

(3) Villages participate in selecting village health workers from among the women of the villages. In this way, villagers themselves determine who shall be the key health agents of health education and services for the entire community. At the same time, the community commits itself to participate with the village health worker to learn health-giving behavior and activity—in short, to support her in her work.

(4) Not only do individuals and families cooperate with the village health worker's initiatives; the village clubs also support her work. Literate club members assist the village health worker with such activities as record-keeping. The clubs encourage the participation of the entire village in eye-screening programs which help prevent the eye diseases which too frequently lead to blindness. Vitamin A deficiency, for instance, is one of the most serious nutritional diseases among young children in developing countries; every year, two hundred fifty thousand children go blind and many others become ill and die due to the lack of dark green leafy vegetables in their diet or Vitamin A tablets.

(5) The work village clubs do to promote education and socio-economic development serves to increase family income and, in turn, pro-

mote health. Poverty and ignorance are clearly two of the primary root causes of ill health in rural areas. The clubs encourage government agencies and banks to support the villages financially so that local industries can be developed and agricultural and animal husbandry processes improved. Such participation with groups outside the village helps correct the uneven distribution of resources between urban and rural areas that has long been a major factor in the perpetuation of poverty among the people of India's vast rural areas.

(6) As the village health worker—usually a woman of low caste, in the caste structure of Hinduism—offers her services to all, social and caste barriers have started to break down. This is another example of new healthful relationships being formed between groups that previously did not work cooperatively because of deep-seated prejudices.

(7) Perhaps the relationship that has brought the most radical change to the health picture in Jamkhed is that between the village health workers and the nurses, paramedical personnel and physicians who work with the Comprehensive Rural Health Project.

When Mabelle and Raj Arole began their work, they knew that even if they worked twenty-four hours a day they would never stem the tide of people already ill who lined up at their door. They realized that unless they could help village people identify and solve most of their own health problems, they themselves would be part of the problem of simply offering treatment and fostering dependency. They knew from experience that although curative and treatment care were desperately needed, these services had to be kept in perspective: they were in demand because the root causes of illness and disease had never been corrected. Little or nothing had been done to keep people from becoming ill in the first place. The Aroles knew that in addition to treatment—and even more important than acquiring new medical technology—work had to be done to enable village people to change the unhealthy living conditions and abject poverty under which they lived.

From the outset, the Aroles focused attention on the tremendous potential of village people. They translated their knowledge and the terminology of health and health care in the people's own language and conceptual framework. They became teachers, counselors and enablers. They taught village people to be the primary caregivers—a job the village health workers have performed so well that the need for more specialized care has taken on manageable proportions.

Our Lord chose simple, humble illiterate people to be His disciples, and through them the message of salvation and eternal life has come to us. He trusted and loved ordinary people and prepared them for this enormous task. He demonstrated that God loves and respects every person we move with. God has endowed every human being with potential.

We are challenged to help persons achieve this potential for their own health and development and for that of the communities in which they live. I believe that primary health care is the greatest challenge to Christian ideals and values. The time has come for the church to take leadership in this vital area of human experience and not to leave human health in the hands of technical experts.

Health for All means that professionals must demystify medicine and simplify medical knowledge so that even illiterate peasants in the countryside can use the principles of medical science to live a healthy life. It means that professionals must act as teachers and catalysts to help ordinary people care for themselves. Health for All envisages people's involvement in identifying their own health problems and their participation in finding solutions. It teaches people to plan their own health strategy and to make proper use of professionals for the betterment of their own health. Health for All and primary health care mean finding and addressing the root causes of ill health by addressing poverty, exploitation, injustice, witchcraft, land tenure, professional greed and the existing value-systems of society.

The church has a great opportunity in joining hands with the national governments who have accepted Health for All as their goal.

—Raj Arole, M.D., Jamkhed

Medical personnel throughout India travel to Jamkhed to observe the results of this new ethic of health care. Through a comprehensive program of health promotion, disease prevention and socio-economic development, the goal of Health for All is taking hold, transforming lives and communities. This has not happened because of what medical care can do, but because of what people can do when they are helped to create healthy families and communities through health-promoting participatory behavior and socio-economic change.

The Aroles have been asked by the Maharashtra State government to extend their work to cover three million people. The task will be done. Again, the key agents will be the village people. Village health workers will train new workers. Already-existing village clubs will provide the success stories to motivate other villages to start such clubs. Across the many hundreds of miles which the Comprehensive Rural Health Project serves, the health promotion message is the same for every person and every village: Health for All means participation.

United States women organize to take charge of their health

Participation that leads to health can take many forms. In the United States, black women, midlife and older women, and urban and rural poor women are coming together in conferences and self-help movements to learn what they can do to protect and promote their own health and the health of their families.

Black women

The first National Conference on Black Women's Health Issues was held in June, 1983, at Spelman College. The conference was inspired by the words of activist and freedom fighter Fannie Lou Hamer, who proclaimed, "I am sick and tired of being sick and tired." The conference was an historic moment in the history of black women. It was designed: (1) to educate black women about health care and health facts; (2) to promote cultural and historical perspectives on the health of black people; (3) to teach self-care skills; (4) to increase awareness of public policies as they impact access to health; and (5) to establish a network among black women.

Fifteen-hundred women from diverse backgrounds, with black women in the great majority, spent three days in dialogue about adequate health care, one of the most critical issues facing black America in the 1980s. The conference signaled the beginning of an organized health movement among black women in America.

The stark realities which the conference addressed continue today, with black women, their children and families bearing a disproportionate burden of suffering, poverty and poor health.

Blacks are the single largest minority group in the United States, accounting for 11.5 percent of the total population and shouldering the highest rate of poverty of any population group. Death from tuberculosis and anemias occurs more frequently among blacks; black women have a 39 percent greater chance of sustaining job-related disease and serious work injuries than nonwhites; though cervical cancer has declined in the U.S. overall, it remains on the increase among black women; diabetes continues at an alarmingly high rate of 34 percent among black women; high blood pressure affects one in four black adults, and its prevalence among women is equal to or greater than its prevalence among black men.

Midlife and older women

Older women are also coming together at conferences to focus on their health needs. Up until now, adequate attention has not been given to helping younger and midlife women avoid the chronic disabilities of older age, although many of these disabilities are preventable. Moreover, problems of aging affect women for a longer time because most women live longer than men.

At midlife and older women's conferences, women are learning that all questions about aging are relevant to them. Among the urgent issues being discussed: How can osteoporosis and strokes be prevented? Can senile macular degeneration, which causes blindness (most frequently in older women), be prevented? Why do the risks of breast and uterine cancer increase with age? What cancers are most likely to affect women at what points in their life cycle, and what can women do to decrease their likelihood? What is the normal, healthy aging process and how can women live in stride with it? How can the psychological and physiological consequences of menopause best be managed, and when, if ever, is surgical or drug intervention warranted?

When Dr. Robert Butler addresses older women's conferences he reminds his audiences that health reflects social conditions. A host of social, political and health strategies are needed in order to extend the prime years of life, enhance their quality, and reduce the duration and intensity of dependency into which too many older women are forced.

The Older Women's League, headquartered in Washington, D.C., was begun in 1980. It is the first and only national membership grassroots organization dedicated specifically to improving the lives of midlife and older women. Working through local organizations and the legislative process, OWL strives to bring about beneficial changes in Social Security, Medicare and Medicaid, pension rights, health insurance provisions and support for caregivers. Over this brief time, the league has translated the concepts of justice and compassion into concrete rights which will positively affect the health, wholeness and well-being of all women.

Rural and urban poor women

The health of urban and rural poor women in the United States also has become an important agenda item in health conferences. In 1984, at West Virginia State College, more than four hundred women from the counties surrounding Charleston, West Virginia participated in a conference at which their health and life situations motivated a call to action. The conference addressed the health effects of persistent poverty, racial discrimination, slum housing, urban squalor and crime.

Urban and rural poor women in the U.S. share a painful common reality with poorer women in developing countries. Poor women everywhere know for fact that health is hard to sustain where poverty and misery abound, where food and safe water are scarce, where unemployment is widespread, where housing is inadequate and where public and community services and education are lacking.

Through health conferences such as these, women are coming together to set a health agenda for the future. Women of color, midlife and older women, women with handicapping conditions and urban and rural poor women are organizing in different regions of the world to usher in a new era of health advocacy and concerted action toward bringing better health for all.

5.   HEALTH FOR ALL MEANS
POLITICAL ACTION

A great scope of issues is affected by political decisions. Health and health issues are poignant examples. As the previous chapters have shown, good health doesn't just happen. It depends on many factors working in favor of women, men, children, families and the communities in which they live.

Of course, health also depends on people taking responsibility for their own health in every way possible. But beyond personal responsibility, health depends heavily on political, social and economic factors.

Political action to protect and promote health

In the chapter "Health for All Means *Prevention*", the reader learned of the situation of Sheila Bond. Though Mrs. Bond is an excellent example of a person who is doing everything within her power to take care of her health, great stress for survival is being placed on her. Chances are good that Mrs. Bond, who is seventy-nine and in fairly good health, will eventually need some type of long-term care. She will soon be a member of the fastest-growing segment of the population, persons age eighty-five and older. The size of this age group is expected to increase five-fold by the year 2050. One in every nine U.S. citizens is presently at least sixty-five; by the year 2020, the proportion will be one in six.

Most elderly Americans who need long-term care are being cared for in the home, often with heavy financial and emotional expense being borne by the caregiver. Mary Day, a sociologist studying the social issues of aging, refers to the aging of the United States population in these terms: "The old are not 'they', they are 'we'. Three decades from now, 'we' will be many millions of Americans."[57]

In 1984, the Physicians' Task Force on Hunger in America found that problems of hunger are getting worse, not better, and that current increases in hunger are the direct result of federal policies. This fact further emphasizes what Gregg Delaney learned in his courses on the politics and sociology of health: there is much more to health promotion than saying people should eat properly; there is also the need to ensure adequate mechanisms which guarantee that people can secure the food they need to protect their health. In this regard, the task force called for strengthening such programs as food stamps, school breakfast and lunch programs, the Supplemental Food Program for Women, Infants and Children, and meal programs for the elderly. Victor Sidel, then president of the American Public Health Association, attempted to get at one of the root causes of hunger by recommending that the government deal with the critical need for programs to ensure full employment for everyone in the United States.

In addition to the larger numbers of persons who are hungry, increasing numbers of persons are uninsured in the United States, where access to health care is not a right. Whether, when and how it will become a right is still in question. A report drafted in 1985 on "The Health Care System in the mid 1990's" reports (among other opinions) that a system with different tiers of care for different persons will be recognized and accomplished. According to the report, "this nation is relinquishing the ideal of full access to mainstream health care for all. The federal government, continuing its retreat from guaranteeing health care, will concentrate on limiting its financial outlays. This retrenchment represents a shift away from the concept that government should ensure equal access to health care for all."[58] By the end of that same year, the percentage of poor and near-poor persons covered by Medicaid had fallen significantly, compared with those covered in the last decade, and private insurance coverage had declined owing to the loss of jobs in manufacturing and other industries. The number of people who have no insurance coverage at all rose from 29 million in 1979 to 35 million in 1985, with the result that one in every six Americans is uninsured or underinsured for medical care.[59] "Today, two-thirds of the 13.3 million children living in poverty [in the United States] are completely uninsured or are insured for only part of the year. Without insurance coverage, their families are in no position to afford the cost of treating a sick infant."[60]

Legislation which affects Social Security, Medicare/Medicaid, pensions, national health insurance, day care centers, nutrition programs, environmental and workplace safety, home health care, long-term care alternatives, job training and employment programs touch on complex social, economic and political issues which influence the health and well-being of all persons.

Health promotion is not something individuals and families can do alone. The success of health promotion and disease prevention depends on a balanced interplay between what individuals can do for themselves and what society must do to protect persons from unnecessary threats to health. Broad-based health promotion efforts and social legislation are needed which will focus on the realities of people's day-to-day lives, where health can be made or broken by social, economic and environmental conditions over which too many people have little control.

Racism, poverty, and health status in the U.S.

June Jackson Christmas, M.D., addressing the First National Conference on Black Women's Health Issues in Atlanta in 1983, pointed to the "troubling" interrelationships which exist between racism, poverty, health care and health status[61] in the United States. Underlying her comments were serious social and health realities. She reminded her audience that blacks not only face financial barriers to health care; they also suffer from those conditions to which poverty contributes. Though only nine percent of white families are poor, thirty-five percent of black families are poor, eighty percent of black people live near poverty and one of every two black children is born into poverty.[62]

At the end of 1985, newspapers carried headlines that infant mortality in this country had fallen to the lowest rate in the nation's history. What most articles did not say was that for America's poor, infant mortality was up; that the "infant mortality rate gap between the rural poor and the rest of the nation grew an alarming 39 percent between 1981 and 1983."[63] Today, black infants continue to die at nearly double the rate of white infants.

In 1985, a task force report on black and minority health further reinforced Dr. Christmas' point, indicating that if the mortality rates for blacks and other minorities were as low as those for whites, more than sixty thousand deaths could be avoided each year.

Accomplishing the goal of Health for All requires that persons of faith be politically and socially aware when they read articles about the nation's health. When one reads headlines about infant mortality rates, heart disease rates, cervical cancer rates or unemployment rates being down, one must ask: down for what groups, but not down for what other groups, and why? When measuring progress in the health of a nation's people it is always necessary to look beneath the national statistics to the information on sub-groups of the population—sub-groups whose health and poverty statistics often differ greatly from those of the rest of the nation.

Health in the United States, like health in developing countries, remains closely linked to income level and to freedom from discrimination which mitigates against health. "Poverty is growing in America and the middle class is no longer secure against poverty. The only thing that keeps millions of households from poverty is that both spouses are now wage earners—not by choice but by absolute need. At the same time that poverty has grown, so has unemployment. The gap between the rich and the poor is larger now than at any time in the past fifty years."[64]

In every country where gross disparities exist between wealth and poverty (whether between racial groups, between men and women, between urban and rural areas) fundamental changes are frequently required to more equally benefit the health of all.

Poverty Rates and Income Inequalities

Census Bureau data released on August 27, 1985 shows that:
• the poverty rate of 14.4 percent in 1984 was the highest since 1966, except for 1982 and 1983;

- *the gap between upper income and low-income American families was wider in 1984 than at any time since Census began collecting these data in 1947;*
- *not only has poverty risen in recent years, those who are poor have grown poorer;*
- *poverty among black children under age six increased again, reaching 51.1 percent; poverty among Hispanic children under age eighteen also rose to 39 percent.*

Income Distribution of American Families in 1984

Population category	Percent of total national income received	Comparison to past percentages
Poorest two-fifths of all families	15.7 percent	Lowest percentage since the Census Bureau began gathering this information in 1947
Middle fifth of all families	17.0 percent	Lowest percentage recorded (since 1947)
Wealthiest two-fifths of all families	67.3 percent	Highest percentage recorded (since 1947)

Source: Bureau of the Census, "Money Income and Poverty Status of Families and Persons in the United States: 1984," August 1985.

According to one UNICEF reporter, "if the drive for better health is to take the road of changes in the lifestyle of the individual, then it must confront the fact that many of the industrialized world's families are living unhealthy lifestyles primarily because they are poor. And at that point it becomes obvious that employment policies, housing policies and basic government services must also be part of any policy which seeks to improve health by changing the circumstances under which individuals live their lives."[65]

Urban wealth, rural poverty and international dependency

In many parts of the world a disproportionate emphasis is placed on urban-centered medical care, in contrast to the health and development work needed by the world's vast rural populations. Yet serious conflicts arise when attempts are made to decrease funds for urban care and to establish national health priorities that support community-based health promotion, disease prevention and socio-economic development.

The attempt to shift priorities away from curative care and toward disease prevention involves the interaction of different social forces. Opposition often comes from those who have access to medical facilities, usually in urban areas, and from those who provide the technology and services that go with it. The first group benefits as consumers from the existing pattern of resource allocation, the latter group as providers. It is sometimes said that mismatching of health needs and health care is irrational, but this is not so. It rationally reflects the interests of all the parties which benefit from things the way they are.[66]

Around the world, courageous Christian health workers are addressing as political and social justice issues the great expense and serious limitations of curative care where the most critical health need is to eliminate the causes of ill health in the first place. The message of these dedicated workers is the same: fundamental political, economic and social changes are called for if Health for All is to be a reality for people who suffer from poverty and oppression.

Sithembiso Nyoni is a rural development worker in Zimbabwe who seeks to bring about fundamental changes in favor of those who live in rural poverty. Following is a brief description of the context within which Ms. Nyoni works and how her work affects the health and development of rural poor people. While reading it, you might ask yourself: In what ways is this situation similar to or different from the situation in North America? How do the foreign policies of the United States (or Canada) and the practices of multinational corporations affect her situation? Ms. Nyoni offers these reflections about urban wealth and rural poverty in her country.[67]

Most of the politicians and the educated people live in cities where the development efforts and services are concentrated. These people live in style, in large individual surburban homes with high fences. They have telephones, private mailboxes and communicate with others who live in the same style. Rarely is there communication across class boundaries. It is common for the top decision-makers to be unaware of the impact of their decisions on the poor because they are too far removed from the day-to-day struggle of these people. Except for occasional visits to village projects, the educated and wealthy have few person-to-person contacts with those who suffer.

Those who have been born and raised in urban luxury do not know what it means to live without water, fuel, transport, food or health care. The children of these urban families no longer die of the same preventable diseases that afflict the children of the poor. The disease patterns of these families are similar to those of families in industrialized countries. High blood pressure, cancer and heart diseases are now common. Most of the health services that exist in the urban centers are a direct response to the needs of these groups and to the market needs of the donor countries who want to supply treatment-oriented medical technologies. Primary health care services and village industries which are so desperately needed in the rural areas have very few resources allocated to them. Therefore what these programs can do in the rural areas is small compared to the problems of injustice and poverty that they are trying to solve.

The politicians and decision-makers decide things every day in favor of the urban centers and large health institutions where only a few can be attended to. They choose to invest in arms instead of agricultural implements to produce more food. They choose to sell the land to multinational corporations to produce such crops as cotton, coffee, tobacco, maize and flowers for export before they distribute land to the rural poor who need the land so they can grow food to feed their own families and to sell for cash. The political leaders choose to export the food in exchange for commercial baby foods and luxury consumer goods.

What is being forgotten and what is being denied in this process is that rural poor families, like all citizens of the country, have a right to food, water, fuel, housing, education, transport, security, income and good health. Political and economic decisions are not being made with the good of all in mind.

Our colonial past and the present influence of capitalism, as well as national and international politics, set the context out of which the poor continue to struggle for human justice, for the equitable distribution of national resources, for the prevention of disease and for health care. There is real need to change the political and socio-economic systems within which all who are poor are trapped. If the lives of the poor are to be different, fundamental change is necessary.

The struggle of the poor, of course, is not just about the disparities between urban and rural areas in the same nation. It is also about the need to break the pattern of international financial dependency. Some African states are aware that large health institutions confined to cities to serve a few people are not the answer. But the aid these states get from overseas donors often dictates what they get and in what form it comes. It may be in the form of drugs or equipment. It depends more on what the donor country wants to give than on what the real needs of the majority of the people are. This dependency is often directly responsible for the underdevelopment of African health resources and services. It is a crippling dependency that makes people look to the outside for solutions rather than developing their own drugs and health organizations. It is essential that countries with po-

litical independence work for economic independence as well, in order to break away from the dependence that ties a country's hands from responding to the real needs of its own people.

Community health and development workers like Sithembiso Nyoni in Zimbabwe and the Aroles in Jamkhed, India are working diligently to bring about the changes which are needed to more equitably benefit the health of all. In their work they are doing what the well-known Chinese verse prescribes: "Go to the people, live among them, serve them, plan with them, start with what they know, build on what they have, learn by doing, teach by showing."

As a result of their approach, these health workers are in direct contact with the hurts and needs of the people. In addition, they benefit from the perceptions of the people—for people themselves can well identify the factors that keep them and their families in need and in ill health. The process is one of two-way consciousness-raising: community people develop skills to analyze their own situation and health workers learn first-hand about the non-medical factors in the community that determine health and illness.

When health is regarded from the perspective of people's lives, it becomes obvious that the task of caring for health must assume a different character from health care as we know it now. Health care cannot be limited to medicine, hospitals, clinics and immunizations. Its concerns must include family incomes, living conditions, land reform, education, human rights, safe environments, national and international economic policies, the effects of transnational corporations on indigenous economies and work forces, the self-determination of peoples, actions that work for peace, and everything that affects human lives.

Through their political action and social involvement, concerned health workers around the world respond to an ominous world health reality: "The causes of ill health—and the things that block the road to good health—are rooted in every part of society . . . and ultimately, in politics. The political and economic changes needed to bring health to all . . . cannot easily be sidestepped."[68]

A worldwide threat to health

Another sign of brokenness which many feel is the greatest threat to the health of the world's people is militarization and nuclear buildup. In 1978, the World Health Organization's Alma Ata Declaration sounded a clear warning: In order to attain an acceptable level of health for all the people of the world by the year 2000, there must be better use of the world's resources, a considerable part of which are now spent on armaments and military conflict. Both in the industrialized world and in the third world, military spending is assuming steadily greater precedence over human needs. In third world countries there is one soldier for every two hundred fifty people, one doctor for every three thousand seven hundred. In 1980, one hundred million people across the world were employed directly or indirectly in the military; this is three times the world's total number of teachers and doctors.

The toll of lives lost and human beings severely injured from the use of atomic weapons on Hiroshima and Nagasaki stands as a constant reminder of the power of nuclear weapons. Today it is estimated that the countries of the world that have nuclear weapons have amassed the nuclear capability to kill all life on earth eight times over.

"If you are inclined to think nuclear weapons are not harmful unless they're used in warfare, talk to the people of the Marshall Islands, whose Pacific atolls were pounded by sixty-six atomic bombs in the nineteen-forties and fifties and where missile tests are now targeted. The story of the Marshall Islands is a dramatic demonstration of the suffering which the nuclear arms race causes quite apart from the potential holocaust of a nuclear war."[69]

My name is Darlene Keju-Johnson. I am from the Marshall Islands, and am thirty-two years old. I remember the night a quarter of a century ago when the sky over my homeland turned bright red. On that night, as with so many other nights since I was born, nuclear bombs were being tested over surrounding islands.

Since then, I have developed tumors in my breast and shoulder. I might never know for sure whether there is any connection between my tumors and the testing of nuclear warheads.

I am a public health worker and an epidemologist and I know about "jelly-fish babies". This is the term used by the women of the Marshall Islands to describe the terrible and often fatal birth defects they believe are caused by radiation from the nuclear fallout. One pregnancy out of every one hundred twenty in the Marshall Islands results in the birth of a baby demonstrating such gross deformities.

The Marshallese people want the world to know what has happened to them. They want the whole church to pray for them and to speak out on their behalf, for health and wholeness. . . . The Marshallese people will be living with the reality of ionizing radiation for a long time to come.

(Dr. Rosalie Bertell, a Canadian biostatistician, and cancer researcher at Toronto's Jesuit Center, reports that twenty percent of the women who give birth to these affected fetuses go on to develop a particularly virulent form of uterine cancer.)[70]

In 1985, the sum of eight hundred billion dollars was spent for armaments by the nations of the world. That sum is more than the total combined income of the people of the countries of the world where the poorest half of the world's population lives.

What might be accomplished if even a small part of that amount were allocated for improvements in the health and well-being of the world's people? The impact would be enormous. The equivalent of three weeks' military expenditures, for example, would provide the fresh water and sanitation needed to overcome the causes of eighty percent of the sickness in the world.

Victor Sidel, in his final address as president of the American Public Health Association, used a metronome to demonstrate how every second of every minute of every hour of every day represents the conflict between basic human needs and military spending.

The metronome is set at a rate of one beat per second. With every other beat, once every two seconds, a child dies of preventable illness, preventable by safe water supplies, basic immunization and basic adequate food supply. With every other beat, also once every two seconds, a child is permanently disabled, physically or mentally, by a preventable illness and is forced to live the remainder of his or her life with that disability. With each beat, in other words, a child is preventably killed or maimed.

And with each beat of the metronome, the world spends $25,000 on military arms. The calculation is easy to remember: the world's annual military spending is $800 billion—that's two billion each day, $100 million each hour, one and one-half million dollars each minute, $25,000 each second. Tiny fractions of that spending could, of course, produce remarkable changes in health. The entire program that eradicated smallpox from the face of the Earth cost less than one hour of current arms spending. The cost of three hours of world arms spending would pay for all of the World Health Organization's (WHO) $250 million annual budget. The cost of one half day of world arms spending could pay for the full immunization of all the children in the world against the common infectious diseases. WHO has proposed a $7.5 billion five-year malaria control program. It represents four days of the world arms race. The most that the world will currently give WHO for malaria control annually is $30 million, 20 minutes of the world arms race. More broadly, the relief from military expenditures could help to free resources for long-lasting public health change, the provision of organized, comprehensive, community-based health services for everyone on the planet. And that relief could help lead the way toward the only real solution to the poverty-based health problems of the poor nations of the world: a new international economic order that would bring an end to the current ravaging of the poor nations by the rich ones.

Of course, the arms that are produced by this debasement of the world's riches, particularly the nuclear arms, themselves pose a severe threat to life and health, a danger that has been described as the "final epidemic". The world now has nuclear stockpiles equivalent to sixteen billion tons of TNT, four tons—not four pounds—for every human being on the planet. If the metronome were counting up the equivalent tons of TNT stockpiled as nuclear arms, it would have to beat at this rate for five hundred years. These arms are capable of causing hundreds of millions of immediate deaths and, through ecological destruction such as "nuclear winter", endangering the very existence of our species. We are the first generation of life on Earth with the capacity to end all future generations.[71]

Working for the health and wholeness of persons and the societies in which they live

Persons of faith are called to realize that health is affected by a great deal more than meets the eye. Many of the things that cause others to be ill are rooted in each of us and in the systems we support. Though the attitudes we hold and the political decisions we make are not identified as causes of disease and suffering as readily as are our personal habits or bacteria or viruses, they are equally virulent and as destructive of the health of the world's people. In James Goldman's play *The Lion in Winter,* the medieval French queen Eleanor of Aquitaine states that it is we who carry within us the seeds of war, the reasons other die hungry and young, the causes of suffering for millions. It is we who by our decisions decide many of these things day by day.

As important as it is for individuals to be concerned about their own health and that of their families, health and wholeness cannot be relativized to personalistic concern without the health and wholeness of all suffering.

The health and wholeness not only of individuals, but of whole societies must be a matter of concern to the church. Churches must not only address the ways individuals' activities promote or impede health, but must be aware of how the decisions and activities of the larger society affect the health and wholeness of persons and their communities.

Today's liberation theologies attempt to unite what has long been separated in religious arenas: concern for the individual and concern for the social and political aspects of life. Liberation theologies remind the churches that they must address the vast collective structures of war, racism, poverty, oppression and exploitation which perpetuate illness, needless suffering and senseless death on a massive scale.

We begin to do this when, in addition to believing that the spirit of God dwells within us, we confess that God addresses us at every moment as social beings embedded in socio-political and economic systems who are called to band together to seek a transformed society capable of promoting and sustaining Health for All.[72]

A faith-inspired response to the goal of Health for All does not personalize the gospel message; rather, it sets persons about the task of establishing love and justice as political, social and economic realities. One thinks of Martin Luther King, Jr., Bishop Oscar Romero, Steve Biko, Sister Ita Ford, Molly Blackburn or the many conscientious Christian health and development workers like Erlinda Senturias, Mabelle and Raj Arole and Sithembiso Nyoni whose lives bear witness to the struggle to create societies in which Health for All can become reality. Theirs are lives of love and servanthood aimed at the liberation of those who are oppressed, poor and in any way discriminated against. It is to achieve more just and compassionate societies in which health and wholeness can flourish that persons are called by faith to live as Jesus taught us.

6. ACQUIRED IMMUNE DEFICIENCY SYNDROME (AIDS)

A Case-Study for Disease Prevention, Participation and Political Action

Late at night, after the traffic outside has quieted somewhat, a young man lies in his apartment on West 16th Street in [the] Chelsea [section of New York City], crying out in pain. Bob Herman, once a promising interior lighting designer, is dying of AIDS.

Herman's mother, Fran, sleeps on a single mattress nearby, and as she listens to him scream she wonders if she can muster the strength to sit with him through yet another night. She always does. But the pain that is shooting through her son's legs and feet is slowly wearing her down too.

"For the past week or two it's gotten incredibly worse," Fran Herman said recently. "He cries. He moans in his sleep. Maybe every 15 or 20 minutes he wakes up screaming with pain."

Five years ago, when the first cases of AIDS were identified in the United States, the presence of parents such as Herman was a good deal less common than it is now . . . many parents abandoned their sons and daughters when they came down with what remains an incurable syndrome.

The Reverend William Doubleday, chaplain at St. Luke's-Roosevelt Hospital, said that "the physical and the emotional . . . are very intertwined, and the visible love and concern of family really does make a difference in the health of people with AIDS." Doubleday said that the family members who are most likely to stick with their children are those who have had some success in communicating with them in the past.

Many of the parents who have cared for their children at home or in hospitals until the end, or who are doing so now, say they never would trade the experience.

"I say it to people who have a question about doing it: Don't deprive yourself of taking care of somebody with AIDS," Fran Herman said. "It is a gift. With all the heartbreak, there is such a wonderful, intimate sharing—such a care and love that develops between two people."

"We often watch TV together, side-by-side, holding hands," Fran Herman said. Bob said, "There are times I just want her there. I just need a human being next to me."

—Newsday, March 17, 1986

In July 1986, Fran Herman became a leader of a support group for mothers of persons with AIDS. Through the shared experiences of pain and caregiving, mothers of children with AIDS are joining together for renewed strength and understand-

73

ing. For an hour and half each week they talk together, reach out, touch, and share in the common reality of loving someone who has AIDS.

The first cases of Acquired Immune Deficiency Syndrome were reported by the Atlanta-based Centers for Disease Control in June 1981. By August 1986, over 23,000 persons had been diagnosed with AIDS, 55 percent of whom had died. As many as 1 million to 1.5 million additional Americans are thought to be infected with the causative virus.

AIDS is characterized by a defect in the body's natural immunity against disease. Persons with AIDS are vulnerable to illnesses that are not a threat to anyone whose immune system is functioning normally.

On June 12, 1986 U.S. federal health officials gave conservative projections estimating that by the end of 1991 there would be a cumulative total of 270,000 AIDS cases in the United States and 179,000 deaths.

Two cities, New York and San Francisco, presently account for over forty percent of the nation's AIDS cases. It is estimated that by 1991 the geographical distribution of the disease will be different, with these two cities accounting for only twenty percent of the cases as the disease spreads more widely across the country.

Countries from every continent are reporting AIDS cases, with significant increases in numbers in Central Africa, Europe, Latin America and the Caribbean. The World Health Organization refers to AIDS as a disease of global proportions.

Who is affected by AIDS?

AIDS is caused by a retrovirus scientifically referred to by the abbreviation, HIV.[73] The disease can be transmitted from one infected person to another by means of intimate sexual contact; contact with infected blood or blood components; by contaminated needles associated with drug abuse; and from an infected mother to her baby before or during birth through blood,[74] or possibly shortly thereafter through breastmilk.

There is no evidence that everyday social or familial contact spreads AIDS. No definitive cure, vaccine or reliable predictive tests for AIDS have been developed.

AIDS can be prevented. Its risks have been substantially reduced for some persons, and there are measures which can be taken to provide greater protection to those most at risk and to the general public.

In 1985, the U.S. Department of Health and Human Services introduced the use of the HIV antibody test to screen the nation's blood supply in the hope of reducing the risk of exposure to the AIDS virus by persons who must receive blood or blood products for medical reasons. In addition, persons who know or think they have been exposed to the AIDS virus are complying voluntarily with the Public Health Services' request that they not donate blood. As a result, the health services reported in 1986 that "only a very small number of additional infections are likely to occur through blood and plasma transfusions."[75]

Health education and disease prevention

In the absence of a vaccine to protect persons against the AIDS virus, public education is the only disease prevention strategy against the spread of AIDS. Getting the message out about how the disease is and is not spread, as well as how to reduce the risk of exposure to the virus, is a critical public health concern.

One of the initial steps in any nationwide public education program about AIDS requires that public officials, health workers, educators, community civil servants and religious leaders be fully informed and respond rationally to this disease. Mass hysteria about AIDS and fear of persons (including children) with AIDS, have been promoted by the misinformation that AIDS can be spread by casual contact. Leaders of public opinion—including religious and political figures—who are reticent to counter AIDS fear with scientific facts do a disservice to the people and the communities which have placed trust in them.

In addition to the need to get correct information to the general public, there is a critical need for specific education that addresses AIDS risk reduction. The effectiveness of efforts to educate individuals most at risk of contracting AIDS has been impressively demonstrated through the efforts of privately and locally funded community groups across the United States. "Unfortunately these programs have reached only a small portion of those at risk and they have generally been implemented only in the major cities."[76]

Urban and rural regions which presently have no or only a few cases of AIDS can benefit greatly from well-coordinated and sustained educational efforts initiated early: the public is informed, unnecessary fear is allayed, and a few cases of AIDS are kept from becoming a community-wide epidemic. Regardless of the present number of AIDS cases in a town or city, general education for the entire public—and specific risk-reduction education designed for all persons who might be at high risk of acquiring and transmitting AIDS—are of inestimable worth to the entire community.

Jeffery Levi, of the National Gay Task Force, testifying before a U.S. House of Representatives Subcommittee in 1985, stated succinctly the task that faces the nation: "The most effective public education programs are those targeted at specific risk groups and run by community-based groups that best understand the target group. Until we can get the information about how to slow the transmission of AIDS to the public—and then work with those at risk in incorporating that information into their everyday lives—we will not slow the spread of this epidemic."[77]

In addition to person-to-person education directed to individuals and groups, information about AIDS can be made available through the mass media, such as public service announcements on radio and television, and through the print media.

In response to the larger issue at stake in the question, "Who is affected by AIDS?", the answer is: "Everyone." Everyone is affected by the propagation of fear and ignorance when scientifically-sound information is not widely available and sought in every community. This education and information must be appropriate—that is, culturally sensitive to the specific needs of those who are at risk of contracting AIDS through specific modes of disease transmission. All groups within a community have a role to play, including the health sector, the educational sector and the religious sector. Health promotion and disease prevention are the responsibility of all groups in a community working cooperatively for the benefit and well-being of all.

In the story of Jamkhed, India, numerous types of health-promoting participatory behavior and activities were outlined. These included the efforts of thousands of individuals to adopt healthier ways of living and take greater responsibility for their own health and for protecting and promoting the health of others. Health education targeted to the specific needs of different groups in the population was a main factor in turning Jamkhed into a cradle of hope and health for all.

Community-wide cooperation and participation

In addition to providing sustained health education programs, AIDS presents another challenge to communities and governments: that of working cooperatively to provide high-quality cost-effective health, social and human services which address the broad-ranging needs of persons with AIDS, their families and loved ones.

Hospital-based medical care is required from time to time by persons with acute AIDS, and there are specific steps hospitals can take to be prepared to offer high-quality care. Education about AIDS and how to care for persons with AIDS must be given to all hospital personnel, medical and non-medical. In this way, fears will be decreased, proper care can be ensured, and an atmosphere of humane caring will be promoted. In addition to hospital care, however, coordinated community and social services are required which are similar to the services needed by persons who have other chronic illnesses.

AIDS helps communities recognize that optimal quality care for persons with serious chronic illnesses requires the existence and effective utilization of a range of cost-effective services. "We've become increasingly sensitive to the fact that, in order to provide good care to people with chronic diseases, we need to deal effectively with social supports, with problems of housing, with problems of income maintenance, with social services, and so on. This implies an entirely new set of relationships between physicians and other health care and service providers, and also implies some very different notions about how to pay for services and how to finance them."[78]

The city of San Francisco has set a sound example of how persons with AIDS, as well as the entire community, can benefit from the provision of comprehensive services. Outpatient clinics, residential facilities and hospice care reduce the amount of unnecessary time persons with AIDS must spend in the hospital. These service alternatives are not only less expensive than hospitals, but they can also be designed to more fully address the wholistic—psychological, social, personal and spiritual—needs of persons with AIDS.

In the past five years, concern over AIDS in the United States has focused attention on a number of problems and unanswered needs. Though these may not be new, they converge to make AIDS the multi-dimensional health crisis it is.

The AIDS crisis raises health policy questions which have long been ineffectively dealt with, and which the United States now must scramble to address. For example, the existence of effective, comprehensive and well-coordinated community-based social, health and human services is sparse. Too few towns and cities in the United States are prepared to provide the full range of coordinated care and services to persons with AIDS which is available in San Francisco. The AIDS crisis also highlights the past and current inadequacy of programs to prevent and treat drug abuse, which is the most rapidly growing mode of AIDS transmission.

In addition, a decline in the value of social solidarity in contemporary U.S. society is demonstrated in the "deterioration of social insurance mechanisms to pay the costs of health care"[79] and to finance the associated social service needs of persons with AIDS and other chronic conditions.

Perhaps like no other health problem today, AIDS presents both a challenge and opportunity for national political leaders to address the United States' larger health care crisis; that of expensive, uncoordinated, under-funded care oriented more toward treatment than to prevention.

The politics of AIDS

In *Illness as Metaphor*, author Susan Sontag writes: "nothing is more punitive than to give a disease a meaning—that meaning being inevitably a moralistic one."[80]

The earliest cases of AIDS in the United States appeared predominately among persons who engaged in behavior which the majority of the population outwardly disapproved of—intimate sexual contact with persons of the same sex, and/or the use of intravenous drugs. As a result, the initial reaction to AIDS was largely characterized by a "blame the victim" attitude. Even after scientists and researchers had identified the AIDS virus as one which could infect anyone, deep-seated personal and social prejudice against homosexual and bisexual men and intravenous drug-using men and women fueled the belief that AIDS was reserved for groups of people who deserved what they were getting.

Six years later, incidences of prejudice and discrimination continue against persons who have AIDS, even against those who are perceived to be at risk. Yet at the same time, AIDS is slowly being recognized as the national public health crisis it is.

The attention of the general public, the public health sector, the health services and health financing sectors, human rights advocacy groups and the federal government has focused on a number of key issues.

Some of these issues offer churches and persons of faith an opportunity to speak out on the side of compassion, fairness, love and justice for individuals, their families and loved ones, and for the communities in which they live.

Two of these issues have already been mentioned: public health education and comprehensive community-based care. A third, related concern has to do with legislative protections which exist already and to which persons with AIDS might be entitled. "In addition to Medicaid, the other major entitlement programs of importance to persons with AIDS are Social Security Disability Insurance and Supplemental Security Income. The Social Security Administration headquarters, which is charged with establishing national standards for disability determination, should proceed with all due urgency to develop a workable definition of disability determination that encompasses all those with AIDS-related disabilities, including persons who have severe AIDS-related complex."[81]

Efforts to include persons with AIDS in these entitlement programs come at a time when cost containment is being achieved, in part, by attempts to "hold the line on", if not actually decrease, the amount of federal dollars being spent on persons whose health and social needs are so great. Compassion and justice require that cost containment not further exacerbate the health and economic situation of persons who are poor. Love and justice require that mothers and children on Medicaid not be forced into a position of competing against the equally-urgent need of persons with AIDS for funds from the same entitlement program.

A fourth key concern relates to the appropriate use of the HIV antibody test, which is designed to "measure for the presence of antibodies to the HIV virus, the virus associated with AIDS."[82] The presence of HIV antibodies means that a person has been exposed to the virus. It does not tell whether or not a person has AIDS—it is not a "diagnostic" test. Nor can it tell whether a person is going to develop AIDS. The use for which the test has been developed is that of screening donated blood and plasma, and "to assist in preventing cases of AIDS resulting from blood transfusions or use of blood products, such as factor VIII, needed by patients with hemophilia."[83]

At the outset, a label was used to prevent any misuse of the test beyond its initial application; it stated: " ' . . . it is inappropriate to use this test as a screen for AIDS or as a screen for members of groups at increased risk for AIDS in the general population'."[84]

Later in the same year in which the antibody test was developed for the sole purpose of screening the nation's blood supply, the U.S. military announced that all new recruits and military personnel would be given the test, and that a negative HIV antibody test result would be required to gain employment in any of the United States' service branches.[85]

Some critics of the military's action rightfully interpreted the Defense Department's move as a crack in the flood wall which could lead to widespread and inappropriate use of the test. Not long after the Defense Department's decision, greater public awareness about AIDS among heterosexuals led lawmakers in several states to introduce legislation which would require couples to undergo blood screening for antibodies to the AIDS virus in order to receive a marriage license.[86]

Early in 1986, the legislative director of the Health Insurance Association of America made a case for using the antibody test to test for AIDS the same way persons are tested for other diseases that affect mortality.[87]

Leslie Strassberg, assistant vice-president of actuarial services for Empire Blue Cross and Blue Shield, has taken notable exception to the opinions of other insurance carriers, stating that "blood tests have no place in the insurance business" and that the industry has a social obligation to make insurance available to persons in risk groups.[88]

Jeffery Levi agrees, emphasizing the same point: "We as a society are going to have to make a clear decision as to whether entire classes of individuals will be denied health or life insurance simply because they fall into a high risk group for AIDS. California, Wisconsin and Florida have made that decision in part by banning use of the antibody test by insurance companies; similar measures will be needed in all other states. If we do not take such steps, millions of people could lose their health insurance—and become dependent on public Medicaid programs, thus increasing even more the public sector's financial burden associated with AIDS."[89]

At present, the HIV antibody test is available through private physicians, most state and local health departments and at other test sites. Many health advocates are concerned that the antibody test already is being used to deny employment, housing, and insurance coverage and benefits to persons who test positive for the presence of antibodies. They suggest that the test should not be used for mandatory or mass screening, but should be available for use on a voluntary basis, with guaranteed anonymity or confidentiality and appropriate counseling for all test users. They make a simple significant case in point.

Used on a strictly confidential, anonymous basis, the HIV antibody test, in conjunction with counselling, has potential to help prevent the spread of AIDS through sexual or IV needle sharing contact. For persons whose blood tests negative for antibodies, counselling can provide education about staying uninfected. For persons whose blood tests positive for antibodies, more sensitive confirmatory tests can be run and appropriate medical contacts established. Counselling can emphasize the importance of steps to be taken to prevent reinfection and virus transmission. Sensitive counselling can also result in voluntary contact notification by the tested individual so that sexual partners and IV drug-using partners can be aware of precautions they can take to further protect themselves and their contacts.

Everyone needs to be well-informed about the nature and appropriateness of the antibody test, what it can and cannot do. We need to work to see that states and localities do not sanction the test for use in ways that are not appropriate with regard to what the findings can reveal.

A fifth key area in which political action is needed has to do with

AIDS funding. The amount of $317 million has been proposed by the U.S. Administration for 1987, a year when tremendous pressure will be on the government to move as expeditiously as possible toward the discovery and testing of drugs to treat and prevent AIDS.

As has already been mentioned, funds are also urgently in demand for general public health education about AIDS and for sustained community-based risk reduction education designed for specific groups in the population.

Jeffery Levi, in his testimony before a subcommittee of the U.S. House of Representatives, stressed the government's responsibility to find cost-effective models of comprehensive care for persons with AIDS. "It is time for the federal government to take its head out of the sand and begin to face the budgetary and human impact of not providing comprehensive health care for persons with AIDS. If the number of cases continues to double every nine to twelve months, we will be paying a tremendous budgetary price for this administration's unwillingness to acknowledge the federal government's responsibility to provide decent health care for its citizens. If the administration will not respond on its own, then Congress should mandate a study of the impact of health care costs on the budgets of the federal government and localities—and assess whether the San Francisco model, or some other, might be more cost-effective and how the federal government might provide incentives, through the Medicaid program or directly, to localities to adopt such a cost-effective model."[90]

At the same time that Levi stressed the need for comprehensive community care for persons with AIDS, he addressed the larger issue that "AIDS must not be focused on at the expense of other diseases that are also taking lives unnecessarily and are in need of increased funding."[91] New funds must be sought out, rather than reprioritizing funds from other Public Health Service activities. The AIDS emergency must not require risking the lives and well-being of others because funds are being directed to AIDS from funds previously set aside for other diseases and illnesses.[92]

The churches and the AIDS crisis

Acquired Immune Deficiency Syndrome is a stark reminder that bacteria and viruses co-exist with human life on this earth, sometimes causing little-understood life-threatening illness and disease. This devastation is a humbling reminder of human finitude and of the preciousness of life, of the infinite value of concerned and caring communities, and of the need for responsible individual and public responses to the presence of a disease which will directly or indirectly touch millions of lives.

No disease in this century has so aroused public fear and prejudice, jeopardizing the personal, religious, social, economic, political and public health responses which are required to address this number-one national health priority.

The AIDS crisis confronts individuals, families, communities and the entire nation with painful realities that call the churches to respond with compassion. The gracious love of God exemplified in Jesus' preaching, healing and teaching challenges the churches to be healing communities. It calls churches to reach out through prayers, advocacy, education and direct service to provide supportive ministries to persons with AIDS, their families and loved ones. God's love also enables Christians to come to a deeper understanding of what it means to be the inclusive Body of Christ, not only bringing healing but being healed in the midst of the AIDS crisis.

Every local church can take responsibility to be informed about AIDS and to be prepared to provide a ministry of caring presence to persons affected by AIDS. Every community has a critical need for balanced, accurate and understandable information about AIDS and how to prevent it through health-promoting behavior and health education. The religious community can join with schools and public health officials to make this information available.

Religious health and welfare institutions and congregations can work ecumenically within their communities to provide coordinated comprehensive health care and social services which meet the broad-ranging human needs of persons with AIDS. State, regional and national church bodies can work ecumenically to seek cooperation between the public and private sectors to develop insurance and funding mechanisms to reimburse facilities, communities and health care providers for the cost of caring for persons with AIDS.

Church leaders, congregations and individuals can oppose homophobia and other prejudices which use the AIDS epidemic to discriminate against persons: They can work through local and state human rights agencies to protect the rights of persons with AIDS, their families and friends.

Congregations can organize letter-writing campaigns asking the administration and Congress to see that adequate funds are made available to develop and test drugs for the treatment and prevention of AIDS and to carry out public health education to stop the spread of the disease.

Because there are communities of persons who are disproportionately affected by AIDS, churches can call upon federal and state governments to allocate AIDS treatment and education funds to the advocacy, health and social service programs which work directly with the affected groups of the population.

All churches can cooperate with the National Council of Churches' Task Force on AIDS, learning and sharing information about the many ways in which congregations are responding to Jesus' ministry of healing by becoming healing communities—the inclusive Body of Christ—ministering to persons with AIDS and being ministered to by them.

7. THE CHURCH AS A HEALING COMMUNITY WITHIN NATIONS AND THE WORLD

It is part of God's mission and purpose for the world to bring about wholeness, justice, good health, righteousness, peace, harmony and reconciliation. These are what belong to the Kingdom of God, and we are to be God's agents working with God to bring to pass all that God wants for the universe. God is liberator, never neutral, always siding with the weak and the oppressed.

When there is injustice, exploitation and oppression then the Bible and the God of the Bible are subversive of such a situation. God is a God of surprises, uprooting the powerful and unjust to establish the Kingdom.[93]

—paraphrase of Archbishop Desmond Tutu

The health and wholeness—the life abundant—that God wants us to have in its fullness refers not only to the lives of individuals. As we have seen, it also refers to a much-desired quality of life within society: the way we are to live in relationship with each other, with the environment, and with God.

The decisions we make that affect the lives of others—the justice and equality that systems either promote or deny; the actions of governments; the actions of churches and Christians in response to the Gospel—all these affect the health and wholeness of individuals, communities, nations and the world.

The quest for health and wholeness is to be taken up by individuals and churches within the context of the very real and broken world in which we live. It is a personal and social, religious and secular quest. It includes concern about access to health care and how to prevent disease and promote health. It involves working for human, social, political and economic conditions that support the basic dignity of being a child of God. In some situations, the movement toward health and wholeness requires systemic changes: more equitable sharing of power and resources, and countries working both domestically and with other nations for peace with justice.

The movement toward health and wholeness cannot be separated from human rights and civil rights movements in which persons strive to achieve freedom from persecution and discrimination. It requires the courage to change and be changed through acts of repentence and reconciliation. It depends on governments protecting and defending the good of all persons and all of creation.

Across the world today, churches and individuals are being tested by their faith—called to do whatever they can in homes, in schools, in corporate offices, in government and in businesses large and small to create and promote those humane and just conditions of life which are the signs of God's kingdom, here and now. In responding to this call, persons of faith enliven the church and create healing communities:

communities which take sides with the oppressed. Which are vessels through which God's liberating powers flow. Which name tyranny and the real possibility of global nuclear destruction as signs of evil in the world. Which move the hearts and minds of men, women and children, societies and nations toward the wholeness, the health for all, the fullness of life, the peace with justice, the liberation, the reconciliation and the unity which are God's will.

Point of focus: South Africa

For black children being born and raised in Christian families in South Africa today, apartheid is the antichrist. Nothing imprints the evil image of apartheid as indeliably as scenes of children being tear-gassed, clubbed, whipped, shot, chased through the streets of South Africa's black townships, hunted out, rounded up and trucked off to detention and prison.

"On June 16, 1976, black schoolchildren demonstrating against inferior education under South Africa's apartheid system were shot and killed by police during a peaceful march through the Soweto township. After the body of Hector Petersen, the first child killed, was carried to his burial, six months of violence followed, claiming nearly one thousand lives. This tragedy became known as the 'Soweto Uprising'."[94]

On June 16, 1986, the tenth anniversary of the uprising, churches in South Africa, the United States and around the world engaged in a "Day of Prayer to End the Unjust Rule of Apartheid". In doing so, they responded to a call that went out to Christians across the world:

Dear Brothers and Sisters in Christ,

Never before in the history of our country have so many millions of Christians in South Africa called upon so many millions of Christians throughout the world to join with them in a day of prayer to please God that the present unjust rule of apartheid be brought to an end, that apartheid and racism in all its forms in all countries of the world be removed and destroyed than on this day . . . a decade after Soweto. On behalf of the millions of oppressed people of our land we of the South African Council of Churches call upon all Christians and adherents of all faiths which equally reject apartheid as a policy which is evil, inhuman and destructive to humankind as a whole, to gather with us on this day in churches and cathedrals, in places of worship and work, in streets and public squares, in homes and offices and factories as people of God, young and old, to pray fervently that God may destroy this evil system and that a just, non-racial, democratic and participatory society may emerge.

We call upon you to bring to God in prayer all those who have died in their courageous resistance to apartheid, all those who have been wounded, detained, tortured, banned or driven into exile in their valiant and determined opposition to this vile system. We equally call upon you to include in your supplication the oppressive rulers and all those who through decades of apartheid rule have enjoyed the fruits of oppression and exploitation that they may openly repent of their attitudes and actions, including those of compliance and sinful compromise, and that they may find the courage to side with the oppressed and the exploited and actively support the step towards a future where the whole country will be liberated and re-united, where ethnic divisions will be rejected and resisted, where the human dignity, rights and responsibilities of all people will be honoured and where the church will truly become a servant church, the body of Christ ministering to the people of God.

May this day of prayer in faith become for all of us a day of hope and of celebration of God's triumph of good over evil, of light over darkness! And may violence cease and peace with justice come to our land.

Your brother in Christ,
C.F. Beyers Naude,
General Secretary of the South African Council of Churches

Today, the martyrdom of the young and the innocent continues. Black children and youth, discontent with poverty and oppression, cry out from the wilderness of injustice. They are a formidable voice of conscience united in opposition to a government bent on violating the dignity and human worth that belong to all as a birthright from God.

Archbishop Desmond Tutu writes to the point of the matter: The Soweto children's protest in 1976 "meant that they rejected the entire apartheid system of legalised inferiority, oppression, injustice and exploitation. They were saying: 'We belong to South Africa . . . we are not going to apologise for our existence. God did not make a mistake in creating us black. Nothing is going to stop us from becoming free; our freedom is a gift from God and not something that whites can withhold or grant as they wish.' That message has gone the length and breadth of our beautiful and beloved land."[95]

When the children of South Africa take to the streets, enraged by the separate and unequal existence forced upon them by the government, their actions are not just political. The desire for liberation is profoundly biblical and theological in a land of oppression, where working for liberation is the "the inescapable consequence of taking the Gospel of Jesus Christ seriously."[96]

The challenge to the church

As a healing community, the church is called to analyze and respond to the root causes of brokenness in the human community—to the forces that impede the health, wholeness and fullness of life that God intends for all persons. Likewise, the church as a healing community belongs to a global faith community which transcends national boundaries. When one nation's government is in complicity with the oppressive government of another nation, persons of faith and churches in both nations are challenged to speak prophetically, imploring their nations to do only those things which will bring justice for all.

In the Kairos Document,[97] South African theologians, both lay and professional, have provided a Christian biblical and theological critique on the political crisis in their country. They offered a challenge to all Christians to join in prayer and involvement. They wrote, " . . . the time has come. The moment of truth has arrived. South Africa has been plunged into a crisis that is shaking the foundations and there is every indication that the crisis has just begun and that it will deepen and become even more threatening. It is the *kairos,* or moment of truth, not only for apartheid but also for the church. We see the present crisis . . . as indeed a divine visitation . . . and call upon our Christian brothers and sisters throughout the world to give us the necessary support in this regard so that the daily loss of so many young lives may be brought to a speedy end."

The prophetic theology voiced in South Africa today is vital to these times. It exposes the hard truth about the inhuman treatment of men, women and children by a government that uses the holy name of God in the preamble of a constitution that makes apartheid the law of the land. The brief twenty-five page Kairos Document makes it clear that religion and politics are inseparable. The God of the Exodus is a liberator, active in the events of human history, and is present in time taking sides with the oppressed against their oppressors.

A first task of the document's prophetic theology was to give a social analysis by "reading the signs of the times" (Matt. 16:3) and interpreting this moment (Lk. 12:56):

The situation we are dealing with here is one of oppression.

On the one hand we have those who benefit from the status quo and who are determined to maintain it at any cost. . . . It is in their interests to introduce reforms in order to ensure that the system is not radically changed and that they can continue to benefit from it as they have done in the past. They benefit from the system because it favours them and enables them to accumulate a great deal of wealth and to maintain an exceptionally high standard of living. And they want to make sure that it stays that way even if some adjustments are needed.

On the other hand we have those who do not benefit in any way from the system the way it is now. They are treated as mere labour units, paid starvation wages, separated from their families by migratory labour, moved about like cattle and dumped in homelands to starve—all for the benefit of a privileged minority. They have no say in the system and are supposed to be grateful for the concessions that are offered to them like crumbs. They are no longer prepared to be crushed, oppressed and exploited. What they want is justice for all . . . no compromise is possible. Either we have full and equal justice for all or we don't.

Peter Magubane

Dr. Mamphela Ramphele at Crossroads Squatter Settlement, Cape Town, South Africa

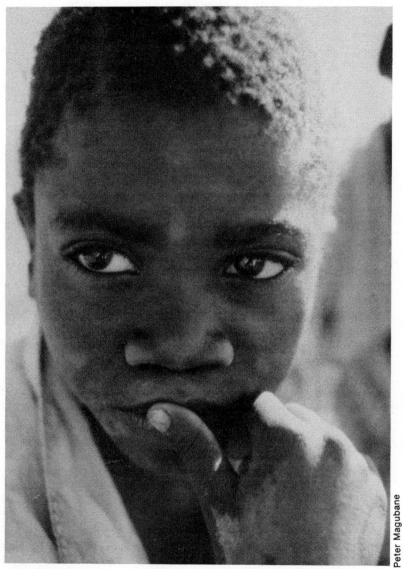

Peter Magubane

What are the churches doing to support the freedom dreams of this South African child and children throughout the world?

This situation of oppression permeates every aspect of South African society over which the government makes decisions. This includes the health and social welfare of people who have no voice or vote in the decisions that rule their lives.

This brutish reality is described by South African physician Mamphela Ramphele in her comments about her country's health care system; it "mirrors the inequalities in society in general", she explains. "The system discriminates on the basis of race, class and geographic locality. Whereas in a normal society resources would be allocated to the areas of greatest need, in our country there is an inverse relationship between need and resource allocation. The poorest are thus the least catered for. . . . Another source of discrimination which has a bearing on the health status of people is the provision of basic needs which is done in accordance with the policy of racial discrimination. The lack of adequate housing, proper nutrition, clean water supply, basic sewerage and waste removal and access to education prejudices the health of those discriminated against by virtue of their race."[98] Dr. Ramphele's critique highlights the day-to-day injustices, oppression and captivity under which the majority of South Africans live and cry out for release.

The message of the Kairos Document is meant to move churches worldwide to side with the oppressed. It stands alongside the writings of other South African religious leaders who implore individuals and churches to take the lead in the struggle for liberation and social justice. "The aim of the Church is to bring about social justice. Justice must be done to the poor and the oppressed, and if the present system does not serve this purpose, the public conscience must be roused to demand another. If the Church does not exert herself for justice in society, and . . . serve as champion for the cause of the poor, others will do it,"[99]—and are doing it. These include the children of South Africa who have taken to the streets defending themselves against the oppression that robs them of their childhood. The Kairos Document is a challenge to the churches of South Africa and the world to listen to these children.

How shall the churches respond?

The black children of South Africa represent an irrepressible public conscience which will acquiesce no further. Their message is clear. But what messages are the churches giving? What are churches doing to support the freedom dreams of these children? What have the churches done to take sides with the God who takes sides?

In 1985, church leaders at national and international levels responded ecumenically, calling for actions in which local churches and persons of faith across the world can participate. The World Council of Churches, at the request of the South African Council of Churches, called an emergency meeting on apartheid, held in Harare, Zimbabwe, from which the meeting's unanimously-adopted Harare Declaration[100] took its name. Over sixty world church leaders came together in December 1985 "to seek God's guidance at this time of profound crisis in South Africa" and committed themselves "to continuing theological reflection on the will of God for the church."

The ecumenical gathering, which included churches from all parts of the world as well as from Southern Africa, affirmed that "the moment of truth (*kairos*) is now, both for South Africa and the world community." The church leaders called for an immediate end to the imposed state of emergency in South Africa; for the release of Nelson Mandela and all political prisoners; for the return of exiles. They offered encouragement to trade unions to continue "collaborative efforts to form a united front against apartheid. Additionally, the Harare Declaration calls upon churches around the world to take decisive actions to assist in bringing an end to apartheid. These actions included calls for comprehensive sanctions, opposition to the renewal of bank loans to the South African government, support for liberation movements and implementation of United Nations Resolution 435 demanding that South Africa quit Namibia."[101]

Having "heard the cries of anguish of the people of South Africa trapped in the oppressive structures of apartheid," the church leaders agreed "that the apartheid structure is against God's will . . . is morally indefensible" and that in view of this, "the South African government has no credibility . . . The transfer of power to the majority of the people, based on universal sufferage is the only lasting solution to the present crisis." In prophetic solidarity, the church leaders from Western Europe, North America, Australia, South Africa and other parts of Africa declared their understanding and full support of "those in South Africa who are calling for the resignation of the government."

Shortly after the Harare meeting, one hundred and twenty U.S. church leaders representing twenty-five Protestant, Orthodox and Roman Catholic churches met on January 13, 1986 at the National City Christian Church in Washington, D.C. and formed the Churches Emergency Committee on Southern Africa. Its task: to speak with one voice in saying *No* to apartheid. And to act to involve congregations in efforts to end apartheid; to coordinate and expand the work of the churches in regard to Southern Africa; to speak with one voice of conscience to the federal government and those who set forth and carry out U.S. policy, urging, among other things, comprehensive economic sanctions against South Africa and the use of moral persuasion to convince U.S. corporations to no longer do business in South Africa.

The prophetic voice of the church leaders gathered at Harare is being echoed in the U.S. by church leaders confessing that "apartheid is an unmitigated evil, the product of sin and the work of the devil"[102] and who, with one voice—on behalf of the churches of America—are calling on all Americans to join in action against apartheid.

Justice: A precondition of health and wholeness for all

Earlier in this book it was mentioned that through the work of churches and religious groups worldwide, new visions have developed which point to health and wholeness as "a dynamic state of well-being of the individual and the society; of physical, mental, spiritual, economic, political and social well-being; of being in harmony with each other, with the natural environment, with God." This dynamic state of well-being cannot be experienced by some while it is denied to others.

God created human beings for one another. God created us to live together in communities which strive to make justice a reality for all. Racism—whether in South Africa or in the personal, institutional and systematic racism that is deeply rooted in North America—denies what God intended.

Archbishop Desmond Tutu writes eloquently about this in his statement "On the Evil of Apartheid":

> The chief work that Jesus came to perform on earth can be summed up in the word 'reconciliation'. He came to restore human community . . . He came to say that God had intended us for fellowship, for koinonia, for togetherness, without destroying our distinctiveness. Apartheid quite deliberately denies and repudiates this central act of Jesus and says we are made for separateness, for disunity, for emnity, for alienation. For this reason alone apartheid is totally unchristian and unbiblical, for it denies not just a peripheral matter but a central verity of the Christian faith.[103]
>
> How is it still possible that such a separation can be preached and lived as the will of God and in accordance with the Gospel?[104]

Beyers Naude's call to Christians of the world church to join millions in South Africa in the June 1986 day of prayer was very specific. Bringing an end to *global* racism, not just to apartheid in South Africa, is to be a part of the work of the churches. That supplication for prayer and action is as real today as it was in 1986. The great need continues for apartheid and racism in all its forms in all parts of the world to be destroyed. The challenge to the global faith community is twofold: to combat racism at home and everywhere it exists.

The United States has a long, ugly history of racial discrimination. Institutional, systemic and personal racism continue in church and society. Its effects are demonstrated in excessive deaths for persons of color, in high unemployment rates, in the perpetuation of living and social situations which interfere with health, place some people at a greater risk of disease, and interfere with growth. "Among black children living in female-headed families, 67 percent are poor; among Hispanic children living in female-headed families, an intolerable 71 percent are poor. Of *all* young children in the U.S., 25 percent—one in four—live in poverty. Of *all* young black children in the United States, over 50 percent live in poverty, the highest poverty rate for black children ever recorded in this rich nation. Yet these data were not even mentioned in the report from the U.S. Department of Health and Human Services on the health status of black and minority people ''[105] published in 1985.

The persistent and troubling interrelationship of racism, povery, health care and health status in the United States must be a critical issue for U.S. churches, even as these churches are called to respond to the crisis in South Africa. The United States' involvement in the perpetuation of racism does not stop at its borders. This is a message the church leaders who met in Harare and in Washington attempted to make clear to congregations across the country.

Communities and nations torn by racism and oppression are not healthy or whole communities. The brokenness of communities and nations is reflected in the brokenness of the human community: in the excessive wealth of some and the abject poverty of others; in one country's national obsession with being thin and losing weight while millions in the same world starve; in the selfish materialistic pleasures of some in contrast to the lives of those who toil endlessly to survive from one day to the next.

One cannot know harmony with God while one is oppressing others—or when one does not speak out against injustices that deny other persons the health and wholeness which is God's will for all of creation.

"It is through a religious act" such as the Exodus and the current challenge to the churches to help end the unjust rule of apartheid and racism everywhere "that people set meaning over against meaningless-ness, wholeness over against being fragmented, courage over against fear."[106] Christians and churches must work to establish just societies where health and wholeness can be realized by all. "Everything has meaning; justice and love are not merely ideas we have concocted, ideas which, if the occasion calls for it, can be replaced by others."[107] Doing justice and love "belong to the unconditional meaning of the experience of wholeness."[108]

The world in which we live as socio-political beings is the place where justice and love are to be done by churches and persons of faith. The work of justice and liberation is central to health and wholeness. To work for the liberation of all persons from that which oppresses them—for the liberation of the oppressor from oppressive ways as well as for the liberation of the oppressed from injustice—is a responsibility given to the followers of Jesus Christ, for whom health and wholeness was a way of life lived loving others the way God loved him.

FOOTNOTES

1. Kenneth Bakken, *The Call to Wholeness: Health as a Spiritual Journey* (New York: The Crossroad Publishing Company, 1985), p. 41.
2. *Ibid.* p. 26.
3. *Ibid.* p. 34.
4. Dorothee Soelle, *The Strength of the Weak* (Philadelphia: Westminster Press, 1984), p. 134.
5. *Ibid.* pp. 135-136.
6. *Ibid.* p. 155.
7. *Ibid.* All following quotes are from Soelle's chapter, "Share your Bread with the Hungry", pp. 153-160.
8. Rosemary Ruether, *To Change the World* (New York: The Crossroad Publishing Company, 1983), p. 20.
9. *Ibid.* p. 19.
10. Desmond Tutu, *Hope and Suffering* (Grand Rapids: William B. Eerdmans Publishing Co., 1984), p. 55.
11. *Ibid.* p. 58.
12. *Ibid.*
13. *Ibid.* p. 59.
14. *Ibid.* p. 60.
15. *Ibid.* p. 59.
16. Rosemary Ruether, *To Change the World*. All following quotes in this section, except where otherwise noted, are from Ruether's chapter on "Christology and Latin American Liberation Theology", pp. 19-30.
17. Dorothee Soelle, *Death by Bread Alone* (Philadelphia: Westminster Press, 1984), p. 35.
18. *Ibid.* p. 134.
19. A Pastoral Letter and Foundation Document to All United Methodists, *In Defense of Creation: The Nuclear Crisis and a Just Peace* (United Methodist Council of Bishops, 1985), pp. 55–59, foreword to the Foundation Document. All following quotes in this section, except where otherwise noted, are from *In Defense of Creation*.
20. Kenneth Bakken, *The Call to Wholeness*, p. 41.
21. *Ibid.* p. 55.
22. Dorothee Soelle, *The Arms Race Kills: Even Without War* (Philadelphia: Fortress Press, 1982), p. 49.
23. *Ibid.* p. 51.
24. Rosemary Ruether, *To Change the World*, p. 11.
25. *Ibid.* p. 15.
26. *Ibid.*
27. *Ibid.* p. 14.
28. Kenneth Bakken, *The Call to Wholeness*, p. 8.
29. Barbara Skolnick, *Prescription for Action*, American Association of Retired Persons, 1984, p. 5.

30. Victor Sidel, "The Fabric of Public Health", *American Journal of Public Health*, Vol. 76, No. 4, p. 374.

31. *Cut the Cost and Keep the Care*, American Association of Retired Persons, 1985, outlines steps to be taken to cut the cost and keep the care.

32. "Indian Alcoholism a National Plague", *NIHB Health Reporter*, Vol. 4, No. 4, June 1986, p. 5.

33. *Ibid*.

34. "The Disparities of Health Status Between Minority and Non-Minority Americans", *American Indian Health Care Association News Briefs*, March-April 1985, unnumbered p. 10.

35. *Ibid*. unnumbered p. 11.

36. "Group Waging Hunger War: Acts to Link Poor with Resources", *The Tennessean*, October 31, 1985, p. 3-8.

37. *Healthy People: The Surgeon General's Report on Health Promotion and Disease Prevention 1979* (Washington, D.C.: U.S. Department of Health, Education and Welfare, 1980), p. 14.

38. Kenneth Bakken, *The Call to Wholeness*, pp. 8-9.

39. *Cut the Cost and Keep the Care*, p. 5.

40. *Healthy People*, p. 36.

41. *Ibid*. p. 103.

42. *Ibid*. p. 106.

43. Helen L. Johnson, *Health for the Nation's Harvesters* (Farmington Hills, MI: Migrant Worker Health Council, Inc., 1985), p. 190.

44. *Ibid*., p. 191.

45. June Jackson Christmas, "Black Women and Health Care in the 80's", Black Women's Health Issues in the *Spelman Messenger*, Vol. 100, No. 1, Spring 1984, p. 9.

46. *Contact*, Christian Medical Commission Magazine, August 1985, p. 9.

47. *The State of the World's Children 1984*, UNICEF, 1984, p. 22.

48. *IPPF Medical Bulletin*, October 1985, p. 1.

49. *Ibid*. p. 1.

50. *A Comprehensive Prenatal Care Campaign Kit*, Children's Defense Fund, 1985, cover.

51. *The State of the World's Children 1985*, UNICEF, 1985, p. 43.

52. *The State of the World's Children 1984*, UNICEF, 1984, p. 4.

53. *The State of the World's Children 1986*, UNICEF, 1986, p. 48.

54. *Ibid*.

55. *Ibid*. pp. 48-49.

56. David Werner and the Hesperian Foundation, "Disabled Village Children: A Part of Primary Health Care," *Contact*, No. 91, Christian Medical Commission Magazine, June 1986, p. 4.

57. Mary Cantwell, "The Ticking Time Bomb of the Aging", Editorial Notebook, *The New York Times*, November 23, 1985.

58. "The Health Care System in the Mid-1990's", The Health Insurance Association of America, 1850 K Street, NW, Washington, D.C.,20006.

59. Dudley Clendinen, "Meeting on Poor and Health Care", *The New York Times*, October 9, 1985.

60. *The Data Book: A Summary.* "Adolescent Pregnancy Prevention: Prenatal Care Campaign," Children's Defense Fund, 1985, preface, p. 2.

61. Black Women's Health Issues in the *Spelman Messenger*, p. 8.

62. *Ibid.*

63. "For America's Poorest, Infant Mortality Is Up", *The New York Times*, October 24, 1985.

64. *The SOS Bulletin*, Winter 1985, Vol. 1, issue 4, p. 3.

65. *The State of the World's Children 1986*, p. 52.

66. *Women and Health: A Women's Health is more than a Medical Issue*, presymposium book prepared for the Symposium on Women and Health, Church Center for the United Nations, New York City, November 9-12, 1983, p. 4.

67. Sithembiso Nyoni, "Political and Economic Factors Affecting Women's Health", unpublished paper presented at the Symposium on Women and Health, Church Center for the United Nations, New York City, November 9-12, 1983. The quoted selection is a paraphrase of material in the paper.

68. Debby Taylor, "The Chance for a Lifetime", *World Health*, (Geneva: World Health Organization) September 1983, p. 11.

69. "Wandering in a Wilderness where Paradise Used to Be", *One World* (Geneva: World Council of Churches) December 1983, p. 11.

70. Cathie Lyons, "The Task of Mending God's Creation", *Women Weaving One World*, 1985 Program Resource, Women's Division, General Board of Global Ministries, The United Methodist Church, pp. 17-18.

71. Victor Sidel, "The Fabric of Public Health", *American Journal of Public Health*, April 1986, Vol. 76, No. 4, pp. 374-375.

72. Rosemary Ruether, *Sexism and God-Talk: Toward a Feminist Theory* (Boston: Beacon Press, 1983), p. 215.

73. HIV is an abbreviation for the Human Immunodeficiency Virus.

74. *Morbidity and Mortality Weekly Report*, March 14, 1986, p. 152.

75. "Tenfold Increase in AIDS Death Toll Is Expected by '91", *New York Times* article by Robert Pear, June 13, 1986.

76. Jeffery Levi, National Gay Task Force Director of Governmental and Political Affairs, Testimony before the Subcommittee on Intergovernmental Relations and Human Resources, Committee on Government Operations, U.S. House of Representatives, September 13, 1985, p. 9.

77. *Ibid.*

78. Bruce C. Vladeck, "The AIDS Crisis: Implications for Public Policy," United Hospital Fund, *President's Letter*, New York, February 1986, p. 4.

79. *Ibid.* p. 2.

80. Susan Sontag, *Illness as Metaphor* (New York: Farrar, Straus and Giroux, 1978), p. 58.

81. Jeffery Levi, Testimony, p. 9.

82. *Ibid.* p. 3.

83. *Facts About AIDS*, U.S. Department of Health and Human Services, Winter 1986, panel 5.

84. Jeffery Levi, Testimony, pp. 3-4.

85. "Military Requires AIDS Test for Recruits, Service Applicants", *AIDS Alert: The Monthly Update for Health Professionals*, January 1986, Vol. 1/No. 1, p. 17.

86. "AIDS-Shy Insurers Turn to Blood Tests", *AIDS Alert*, February 1986, Vol. 1/No. 2, p. 43.

87. *Ibid.*

88. "AIDS-Shy Insurers Turn to Blood Tests", p. 44.

89. Jeffery Levi, Testimony, p. 5.

90. *Ibid.* p. 10.

91. *Ibid.* p. 6.

92. *Ibid.*

93. Desmond Tutu, *Hope and Suffering*, p. 177.

94. "A Moment of Decision", bulletin cover prepared by the Lutheran World Ministries, 360 Park Avenue, New York City, for the June 16, 1986 World Day of Prayer and Fasting to End the Unjust Rule in Southern Africa.

95. Desmond Tutu, "The Impact of the Soweto Riots", *Crying In The Wilderness: The Struggle for Justice in South Africa* (Grand Rapids: William B. Eerdmans Publishing Company, 1982), p. 93.

96. Desmond Tutu, *Hope and Suffering*, p. 76.

97. *The Kairos Document: Challenge to the Church—A Theological Comment on the Political Crisis in South Africa*, published by the Kairos Theologians, P.O. Box 32047, Braamfontein 2017, South Africa. All subsequent quotes in this section on "The challenge to the church," except otherwise footnoted, are from this 25-page document.

98. Mamphela Ramphele, "Health and Social Welfare in South Africa Today", unpublished paper, p. 2.

99. Statement of Reverend C.D. Brink in Desmond Tutu, *Hope and Suffering*, p. 175.

100. For the Harare Declaration, see *ENGAGE/Social Action*, May 1986, p. 11. All subsequent quotes in this section on "How shall the churches respond?," unless otherwise footnoted, are from the Harare Declaration.

101. Harold Massey, "Southern Africa Is Dying for Freedom", *ENGAGE/Social Action*, May 1986, p. 8.

102. "With One Voice", statement approved January 13, 1986 by United States Protestant, Orthodox and Roman Catholic church leaders meeting at the National City Christian Church, Washington, D.C. on Harare follow-up, available from the Churches Emergency Committee on Southern Africa, Rm. 612, 475 Riverside Drive, New York City 10015 (212/870-2645).

103. Desmond Tutu, *Hope and Suffering*, pp. 166-167.

104. Quote of Professor J. Durand in *Hope and Suffering*, p. 167.

105. Victor Sidel, "The Fabric of Public Health", p. 374.

106. Dorothee Soelle, *Death by Bread Alone, p. 130.*

107. *Ibid.* p. 138.

108. *Ibid.*